BASIC LIFE SUPPORT

Comprehensive Handbook of Emergency Cardiovascular Care and CPR

2025-2026 Provider Manual

Dr. Aaliyah Ramdeen

TEKHEALTH
TECHNOLOGY IS YOUR HEALTH

Dr. Aaliyah Ramdeen

Basic Life Support (BLS): Comprehensive Handbook of Emergency Cardiovascular Care and CPR.

Editors

Dr. Marcus B. Antoine

Dr. Nia Baptiste

ISBN: 978-9-3404-4869-7

TekHealth

Printed in the United States of America

CONTENTS

CHAPTER ONE

Introduction to Basic Life Support (BLS)

Basic Life Support (BLS) is a set of essential skills and practices used by healthcare providers and trained individuals to manage life-threatening emergencies until advanced medical care becomes available. At its core, BLS is focused on preserving life, preventing further harm, and promoting recovery by maintaining an open airway, supporting breathing, and ensuring effective circulation in patients experiencing cardiac arrest or other critical medical conditions. These skills can be employed in a wide variety of settings—from hospitals and clinics to public spaces and homes—making BLS an invaluable part of community health and emergency response systems.

The importance of BLS cannot be overstated. Rapid intervention during cardiac arrest, choking, or respiratory distress can mean the difference between life and death, as each minute without intervention dramatically reduces a patient's chances of survival. BLS not only empowers healthcare providers, but it also equips laypeople with the confidence and skills necessary to act swiftly in critical moments. Techniques such as high-quality chest compressions, proper ventilation, and the use of an automated external defibrillator (AED) form the foundation of BLS training, ensuring that responders can perform life-saving actions effectively.

Furthermore, BLS training emphasizes the importance of the Chain of Survival—a series of steps that, when followed, optimize a patient's likelihood of survival in cardiac events. Each link in the Chain of Survival, from early recognition and calling for help to post-resuscitation care, reinforces the collaborative nature of BLS and the crucial role every individual plays in emergency care. BLS providers are also trained to assess scenes for safety, recognize early signs of cardiac or respiratory distress, and deliver interventions while minimizing risks to both patients and themselves.

The latest BLS guidelines, updated based on recent research and best practices, incorporate advances in resuscitation science to maximize positive outcomes in diverse situations. These guidelines emphasize the importance of high-performance CPR, effective teamwork, and adaptability to various patient needs, including special considerations for pediatric, trauma, and high-risk populations. By focusing on standardized techniques and evidence-based practices, BLS not only improves immediate survival rates but also enhances long-term recovery for those who experience life-threatening medical emergencies. BLS training remains an essential component of modern emergency care, empowering communities and healthcare professionals alike with the tools and knowledge to make a lifesaving impact.

SECTION I

Key Concepts and Scope of BLS

The *key* concepts of Basic Life Support (BLS) center on immediate and effective interventions to support and stabilize individuals experiencing cardiac arrest, respiratory arrest, or other life-threatening emergencies until advanced medical care becomes available. BLS involves techniques and skills that are foundational in emergency medicine, designed to prioritize preserving life, preventing further harm, and creating conditions for recovery. These core interventions focus on maintaining an open airway, ensuring effective breathing and oxygenation, and promoting circulation through chest compressions and ventilation. BLS is not limited to healthcare providers; it also encompasses trained lay rescuers, empowering them to respond to emergencies in everyday settings, from homes to workplaces to public spaces.

A critical concept within BLS is the Chain of Survival , which outlines a series of essential actions that must occur quickly and in sequence to optimize a patient's chances of survival during cardiac emergencies. The Chain of Survival consists of five links: recognizing cardiac arrest and activating emergency response, performing high-quality CPR, rapid defibrillation, effective advanced life support, and post-resuscitation care. Each link in this chain depends on rapid response and precision in delivering care, as every moment in an emergency can affect the outcome significantly. The effectiveness of BLS is closely tied to the responder's ability to understand and execute these steps without delay or error.

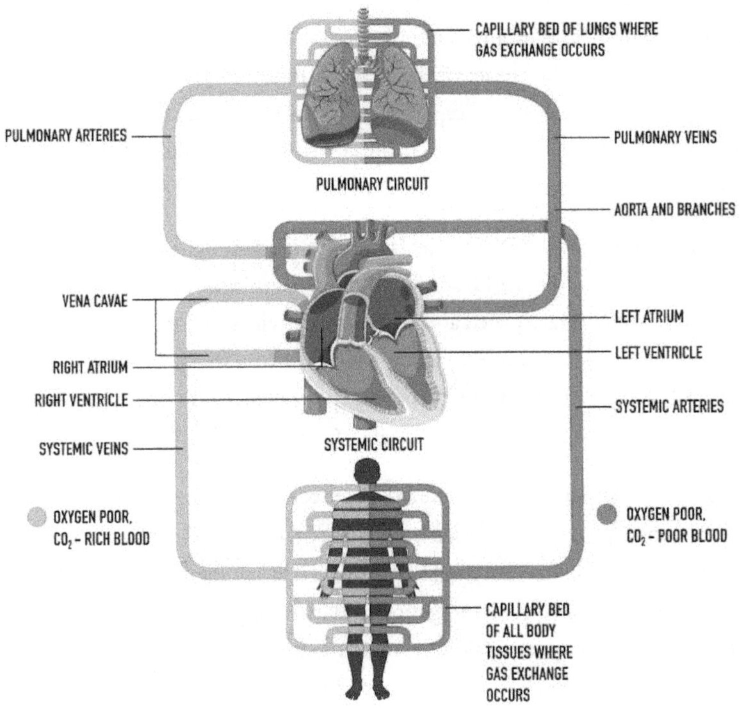

Fig 1. Heart and Lungs Blood flow

BLS encompasses several key skills and techniques that are adaptable to various patient populations, including adults, children, and infants. These techniques include high-quality chest compressions—ensuring the proper depth, rate, and minimal interruptions—along with effective ventilation techniques to supply oxygen to the lungs. The use of automated external defibrillators (AEDs) is also a primary element of BLS, enabling non-medical rescuers to deliver life-saving shocks when ventricular fibrillation or pulseless ventricular tachycardia is present. Through practical training, BLS providers learn to apply AEDs quickly and safely, integrating this crucial step into the broader resuscitative effort.

The *scope* of BLS is designed to be both specific and expansive, covering a variety of medical emergencies where time-sensitive, immediate action is necessary. While cardiac arrest is a primary focus, BLS also addresses management of airway obstructions, recognizing and relieving choking in adults, children, and infants, and adapting CPR techniques based on age and physiological differences in patients. Additionally, BLS training incorporates scene safety assessment to ensure that rescuers remain protected while providing care, emphasizing the principle of doing no further harm to both patients and responders.

An integral part of the BLS scope is training in team dynamics and communication. Many BLS scenarios require multiple providers to work together, often in fast-paced and high-stress environments. Training reinforces the roles of each team member, ensuring that every provider knows how to communicate effectively, perform tasks in sync, and switch roles as needed to maintain high-quality CPR and other interventions.

BLS training is periodically updated to reflect the latest resuscitation science, incorporating evidence-based best practices and innovative techniques to enhance outcomes. Through these guidelines, BLS providers learn to address common emergency scenarios, respond to special situations, and adapt their skills to meet the unique needs of patients with underlying health conditions, traumatic injuries, or specific environmental challenges. The broad but focused scope of BLS ensures that providers can deliver high-impact care in critical moments, bridging the gap between emergency onset and advanced medical intervention.

SECTION II

Roles and Responsibilities of BLS Providers

BLS providers play a critical role in the emergency response chain, bridging the gap between initial recognition of a medical crisis and the arrival of advanced care. Their primary responsibility is to act quickly and competently to provide immediate care for patients experiencing life-threatening events, such as cardiac arrest, respiratory failure, or choking. A BLS provider's actions are centered on the essential objectives of Basic Life Support: ***preserving life, preventing deterioration, and promoting recovery***.

One of the first responsibilities of a BLS provider is to assess the situation for both scene safety and patient condition. Ensuring that the environment is safe for both the patient and the provider is essential, as entering an unsafe scene could result in additional harm. After confirming the safety of the scene, the provider assesses the patient's responsiveness, breathing, and pulse, and quickly determines the most appropriate intervention.

Upon recognizing cardiac arrest or severe respiratory distress, a BLS provider is trained to initiate high-quality CPR promptly. This involves performing chest compressions at the correct depth and rate to maintain circulation of oxygenated blood to vital organs. High-quality compressions are vital, as each compression helps to sustain the patient's life until advanced care can take over. Proper CPR techniques—such as ensuring full recoil between compressions and minimizing interruptions—are practiced to optimize blood flow and improve the patient's chances of survival. In cases where a trained BLS provider has access to a barrier device or other equipment, they may perform rescue breathing to support the patient's oxygenation needs.

In many cardiac arrest situations, using an Automated External Defibrillator (AED) is also within the scope of BLS providers. Providers must be able to rapidly deploy and operate the AED, delivering a shock if advised by the device. The AED's shock can correct an irregular heart rhythm and is a critical intervention for improving survival outcomes in sudden cardiac arrest. BLS providers must also be vigilant in maintaining a calm and organized environment around the patient, creating space for resuscitative efforts, and guiding bystanders if necessary.

Communication and collaboration with other responders and emergency personnel are also essential responsibilities. BLS providers often work as part of a team, particularly in healthcare settings, where coordinated efforts maximize resuscitation success. When additional trained providers arrive, the BLS provider must be prepared to transfer care efficiently and communicate critical details about the patient's condition and the actions taken thus far. In settings with more than one responder, BLS providers may rotate roles to prevent fatigue and sustain high-quality compressions and ventilation.

Additionally, BLS providers are responsible for adhering to the latest BLS protocols and guidelines. The medical and resuscitation fields are constantly evolving based on new research, so staying current with best practices ensures that each provider can deliver the highest standard of care. This commitment to continued learning and skill practice is essential, as it not only improves individual competency but also enhances community-wide preparedness for emergencies.

In specific situations, such as those involving children, infants, or trauma patients, BLS providers must adapt their techniques to the unique needs of these patients. This could mean modifying the depth and rate of compressions or using specialized airway maneuvers. BLS providers are also taught to handle common complications like choking and airway obstruction. The ability to recognize and clear a blocked airway in adults, children, and infants is a vital skill, as obstructions can escalate quickly into respiratory arrest.

Ultimately, the role of a BLS provider is not only to intervene in critical moments but to serve as a first responder who can stabilize and support patients through life-threatening situations. Their responsibilities encompass technical skill, quick judgment, effective communication, and a strong dedication to patient safety and care quality. By mastering these core skills and principles, BLS providers are empowered to make a substantial difference in survival outcomes for patients in emergencies.

SECTION III

Latest BLS Guidelines

The latest Basic Life Support (BLS) guidelines, updated to reflect the most current research and practices, are designed to enhance survival rates and recovery outcomes for patients experiencing life-threatening emergencies, especially cardiac arrest. These guidelines incorporate advancements in resuscitation science and place a stronger emphasis on the quality of interventions, teamwork, and adaptability to different emergency situations.

Key updates and best practices in the latest BLS guidelines:

1. High-Quality CPR

High-quality chest compressions remain the foundation of BLS. The guidelines recommend a compression rate of 100–120 compressions per minute with a depth of at least 2 inches (5 cm) for adults, while allowing the chest to fully recoil between compressions. This depth and rate balance the need for effective blood flow without causing harm to the patient. For children and infants, compression depth and rate are slightly modified to accommodate smaller bodies, but high-quality CPR remains a universal priority across age groups.

2. Minimizing Interruptions in Compressions

Studies show that interruptions in chest compressions can reduce survival rates. The latest guidelines emphasize minimizing pauses during CPR by limiting interruptions to under 10 seconds. This focus includes pausing only when absolutely necessary, such as for defibrillation or switching providers in multi-responder situations. The goal is to ensure continuous blood flow to vital organs, primarily the brain and heart.

3. Ventilation Techniques

In adult BLS, the guidelines recommend rescue breaths in addition to compressions when possible. This should be performed at a ratio of 30 compressions to 2 breaths for a single provider. For children and infants, the ratio remains the same for a single rescuer but adjusts to 15 compressions to 2 breaths when multiple rescuers are available. Proper ventilation is crucial, but the guidelines prioritize chest compressions over ventilation in cases where providing breaths is difficult or delayed.

4. Updated AED Use

The guidelines continue to highlight the importance of early defibrillation with an automated external defibrillator (AED), but they also address specific modifications in AED usage. Providers should apply the AED as soon as it is available, and the device should be placed and activated promptly to deliver shocks when indicated. Training now includes steps to troubleshoot AED errors and ensure electrodes are placed correctly to avoid delays during defibrillation.

5. Pulse Checks and Rhythm Assessment

To enhance response efficiency, providers are instructed to check for a pulse only if they are well-trained in this technique and to limit pulse checks to 10 seconds or less. If no pulse is detected within this window, compressions should begin immediately. Pulse checks and rhythm assessments should also be minimized to prevent unnecessary pauses in chest compressions, with a focus on rapidly transitioning back to CPR if the patient's condition requires it.

6. Special Considerations for Pediatric and Infant BLS

The updated guidelines provide specific instructions tailored to children and infants, recognizing that their anatomical and physiological needs differ from adults. Chest compression techniques and ventilation approaches are adjusted to align with age-appropriate standards, including modified hand placement for compressions and a focus on gentle yet effective ventilation. The latest updates underscore the need for trained responders to understand and apply these distinctions in pediatric emergencies.

7. Team Dynamics and Communication

Effective BLS requires cohesive teamwork and clear communication, especially in multi-provider scenarios. The latest guidelines introduce frameworks for assigning roles, coordinating tasks, and enhancing the flow of care within a team. This includes training on leadership roles, situational awareness, and concise messaging to ensure a high-performance BLS approach that reduces confusion and maximizes the effectiveness of each provider's actions.

8. Adaptations for Special Populations and Scenarios

The guidelines address modifications for populations such as pregnant women, trauma patients, and individuals with obesity, as well as unique situations like drowning or opioid overdose. For example, in cases of opioid overdose, BLS now includes recommendations for the use of naloxone alongside traditional CPR. For pregnant patients, specialized techniques are taught to reduce pressure on the vena cava and to optimize blood flow during resuscitation.

9. Emphasis on Training, Skills Retention, and Recertification

Finally, the guidelines underscore the importance of ongoing training, skills retention, and recertification for BLS providers. The emphasis is on regular practice and updated training to ensure that providers are prepared to deliver high-quality CPR and other BLS interventions confidently and effectively in real-world emergencies.

These latest BLS guidelines aim to optimize patient outcomes by improving the consistency and quality of life-saving interventions across diverse situations. By following these evidence-based practices, BLS providers can maximize survival rates and better support recovery in critical moments.

CHAPTER TWO
Foundational Skills for BLS

SECTION I
Understanding the Chain of Survival

The Chain of Survival is a critical concept in emergency care that outlines the essential steps needed to maximize a patient's chance of survival after a sudden cardiac arrest (SCA) or other life-threatening medical emergencies. It is a series of actions that must be performed in a timely and coordinated manner to provide the best possible outcome for the patient. Understanding and implementing the Chain of Survival is essential for both healthcare professionals and laypeople trained in Basic Life Support (BLS).

1. Early Recognition and Activation of Emergency Medical Services (EMS)

The first link in the Chain of Survival is the early recognition of a life-threatening emergency and the immediate activation of emergency medical services (EMS). Recognizing a sudden cardiac arrest or other critical conditions, such as choking or severe bleeding, is the first step in initiating the chain of events that could save a life. The earlier someone can identify the problem, the sooner help can be activated. In cases like cardiac arrest, this is done by calling emergency services (911 or the local emergency number). Early recognition is crucial because it prompts a rapid response, which increases the chances of survival.

2. Early CPR (Cardiopulmonary Resuscitation)

The second link emphasizes the importance of performing high-quality CPR as soon as possible after the emergency is recognized. CPR involves chest compressions and, if trained, rescue breathing. High-quality chest compressions are vital as they help to maintain blood flow to the heart and brain, preserving vital organs until more advanced care can take over. Early CPR, especially chest compressions, helps to circulate oxygenated blood throughout the body, buying crucial time for the patient. It is important to perform CPR correctly, focusing on the depth and rate of chest compressions to ensure optimal circulation.

3. Early Defibrillation

The third link in the Chain of Survival is the early use of an Automated External Defibrillator (AED). Sudden cardiac arrest often occurs when the heart's electrical system malfunctions, causing irregular rhythms like ventricular fibrillation or pulseless ventricular tachycardia. These rhythms can be corrected with the use of a defibrillator, which delivers an electric shock to restore a normal heart rhythm. AEDs are designed to be used by lay responders as well as healthcare professionals, and their availability in public spaces has been shown to significantly improve survival rates. Prompt use of an AED within minutes of collapse greatly enhances the chances of survival and reduces long-term damage.

4. Effective Advanced Care

The fourth link is the provision of effective advanced care, which typically involves paramedics or emergency medical technicians (EMTs) who arrive on the scene. These professionals are trained to provide advanced interventions, such as intubation to secure the airway, administering medications, and using specialized equipment like advanced cardiac monitoring. This stage is where advanced techniques and expertise come into play to stabilize the patient and prepare them for transport to a healthcare facility for ongoing care.

5. Post-Resuscitation Care and Recovery

The final link in the Chain of Survival is post-resuscitation care, which involves managing the patient's condition after they have been stabilized. This phase includes transporting the patient to a hospital for definitive care, ongoing monitoring, and treatment. The goal is to optimize the chances of survival and minimize the risk of brain injury or other complications. Post-resuscitation care focuses on stabilizing the patient's vital signs, managing underlying causes of the arrest, and preparing for long-term recovery.

The effectiveness of the Chain of Survival depends on the timely and coordinated actions of those involved. Each link is interdependent, meaning that a delay in any one step reduces the likelihood of a successful outcome. Therefore, a fast and efficient response is crucial to ensuring the best possible chance of survival for individuals experiencing a medical emergency. Additionally, the Chain of Survival emphasizes the need for community awareness, training, and the availability of life-saving equipment, like AEDs, in public spaces.

In summary, understanding the Chain of Survival is essential for anyone involved in emergency care. It reinforces the importance of early intervention, whether through recognizing the emergency, performing CPR, using an AED, or providing advanced medical care. Following these steps can dramatically improve outcomes in critical situations and significantly increase the likelihood of survival for individuals experiencing cardiac arrest or other life-threatening emergencies.

SECTION II

Recognizing Sudden Cardiac Arrest

Recognizing sudden cardiac arrest (SCA) is a critical skill for both healthcare providers and bystanders, as it is the first step in initiating life-saving interventions. Sudden cardiac arrest occurs when the heart unexpectedly stops beating due to a malfunction in the electrical system, leading to an immediate cessation of blood circulation to vital organs, particularly the brain and heart. Recognizing SCA early can significantly increase the chances of survival, as the effectiveness of subsequent interventions, such as cardiopulmonary resuscitation (CPR) and defibrillation, greatly depends on how quickly they are initiated.

Sudden cardiac arrest may happen without warning or with very few initial signs, making its recognition challenging. However, certain symptoms and indicators can help a trained or attentive person identify SCA quickly.

The key signs of sudden cardiac arrest include:

1. Collapse or Loss of Consciousness

The most immediate and noticeable sign of SCA is a sudden collapse or loss of consciousness. The person will typically fall to the ground and may not respond to verbal cues or gentle shaking. This collapse occurs because the heart is no longer pumping blood to the brain, causing the person to lose consciousness rapidly. Without the heart's ability to pump blood effectively, the brain is deprived of oxygen, resulting in unconsciousness within seconds.

2. Absence of Normal Breathing

Once cardiac arrest occurs, the individual will stop breathing or may exhibit abnormal, irregular, or agonal breathing (gasping or irregular, shallow breaths). It's important to note that agonal breathing is not a sign of life and should not be confused with normal breathing. In some cases, a person may still have weak or irregular gasps, but these breaths do not supply enough oxygen to sustain life and are often a sign of severe distress. If there is no normal breathing or if breathing is irregular, it is an immediate indication that the person may be experiencing SCA.

3. Absence of a Pulse

A key indicator of sudden cardiac arrest is the absence of a pulse. When the heart stops beating, blood circulation is halted, and the person will not have a detectable pulse in major arteries, such as the carotid artery (on the neck) or the femoral artery (in the groin). Checking for a pulse is an essential step for healthcare professionals and trained bystanders to confirm the presence of cardiac arrest. The absence of a pulse further confirms the need for immediate CPR and defibrillation.

In some cases, there may be no obvious warning signs, making the situation even more critical. SCA can occur unexpectedly, even in individuals who seem healthy or have no known heart disease. However, certain risk factors and conditions can predispose individuals to a higher risk of experiencing SCA, such as:

- **Heart disease**, particularly coronary artery disease
- **Arrhythmias**, like ventricular fibrillation or ventricular tachycardia
- **Electrolyte imbalances**, such as low potassium or magnesium levels
- **Family history** of sudden cardiac arrest or other heart conditions
- **Previous heart attacks** or heart failure
- **Drug use**, including cocaine or certain medications that affect the heart's electrical system
- **Trauma** or severe injury to the chest, which can damage the heart

In some cases, a person may experience warning signs of a heart problem before SCA occurs. These signs might include chest pain, dizziness, shortness of breath, or nausea, which can be early indicators of an impending cardiac event. However, many people may not experience these symptoms before experiencing SCA, highlighting the importance of being vigilant for other signs, such as sudden collapse and loss of consciousness.

The ability to recognize sudden cardiac arrest and act quickly is paramount in improving the chances of survival. Immediate intervention, including performing CPR and using an automated external defibrillator (AED) when necessary, can dramatically increase the likelihood of survival by maintaining circulation to vital organs and restoring a normal heart rhythm.

In summary, recognizing sudden cardiac arrest involves identifying a sudden collapse, the absence of normal breathing, and the absence of a pulse. These signs should trigger immediate action to activate emergency services and begin CPR. Early recognition and intervention are essential, as they are directly linked to the chances of survival, particularly when combined with timely defibrillation using an AED. The faster these actions are taken, the higher the likelihood of a positive outcome, reinforcing the critical importance of recognizing SCA early in an emergency.

SECTION III

Assessing Scene Safety and Personal Protection

Assessing scene safety and personal protection are fundamental steps in any emergency situation, particularly for Basic Life Support (BLS) providers. Before taking any action to assist a victim, it is crucial to ensure that the environment is safe for both the responder and the patient. Inadequate attention to scene safety can lead to further harm or injury, which may worsen the situation or hinder effective care. This principle is vital not only for medical personnel but also for any bystanders attempting to assist in an emergency.

The first step in assessing scene safety is to evaluate the environment quickly and systematically to identify potential hazards. This includes looking for anything that could pose a danger to yourself, the patient, or others nearby. Common hazards might include traffic accidents, fire, unstable structures, electrical wires, or toxic fumes. Each of these presents immediate risks, so a responder must first ensure that the area is free of danger before proceeding.

When assessing the safety of the environment, responders should consider the following:

- **Environmental Hazards:** Check for potential threats such as spilled chemicals, smoke, fire, or gas leaks. If any of these hazards are present, it may be necessary to call for specialized emergency services (e.g., fire department, hazardous materials team) before attempting to assist the patient.

- **Traffic and Roadway Hazards:** If the scene involves a traffic accident or a situation near a road, there is a risk of additional collisions. In such cases, it is essential to stay clear of moving vehicles or traffic lanes. If possible, try to move the victim to a safer location, but only if it is safe to do so without causing harm.

- **Physical Hazards:** These may include things like unstable structures (e.g., collapsed buildings), falling debris, or aggressive individuals. If there is any uncertainty about the safety of the surroundings, it is best to wait for first responders or law enforcement to assess the risk before proceeding.

- **Weather Conditions:** Weather can sometimes create hazardous conditions, such as flooding, lightning, or extreme temperatures. BLS providers must be aware of environmental factors like storms, rain, or heatwaves that could pose a danger to themselves or the patient.

Once the environment has been assessed for dangers, the next consideration is ensuring personal safety. Personal protection is crucial to prevent harm or exposure to the responder while providing care. Various risks, such as exposure to bloodborne pathogens, bodily fluids, or infectious diseases, require precautions to protect both the provider and the patient. The following personal protection measures should be employed:

1. Use of Personal Protective Equipment (PPE)

PPE is designed to provide a barrier between the responder and potential hazards, including infectious materials, bodily fluids, or hazardous substances. Common PPE includes gloves, masks, eye protection, and gowns. When approaching a patient, it is essential to use gloves at a minimum to protect against direct contact with blood or bodily fluids, which can transmit infections. In situations where there is a risk of airborne pathogens, such as when performing rescue breathing, a mask or face shield should be used. In high-risk environments, like hospitals or areas with potential exposure to bloodborne diseases, additional protective gear like gowns, face shields, or goggles may be necessary.

2. Hand Hygiene

Proper hand hygiene is one of the simplest and most effective ways to prevent the transmission of infectious diseases. Before and after using personal protective equipment (PPE) or providing care, it is important to wash hands thoroughly with soap and water or use alcohol-based hand sanitizers. This practice reduces the risk of cross-contamination and protects both the responder and the patient from potential infections.

3. Cautious Handling of Medical Instruments and Materials

In situations where medical instruments, such as scissors, airway devices, or AED pads, are used, it is crucial to ensure that these tools are sterile or disinfected before use. This minimizes the risk of introducing infections to the patient. If the BLS provider is using any invasive procedures (such as suctioning or inserting an airway device), they should ensure that all equipment is properly sterilized and, if necessary, disposable items are used to prevent cross-contamination.

4. Precautions with Blood and Bodily Fluids

Exposure to blood and bodily fluids, such as vomit, saliva, or urine, can carry infectious agents like HIV, hepatitis, and other pathogens. In cases where bodily fluids are present, extra caution is necessary. Always assume that any fluid could potentially be contaminated, and wear appropriate PPE. A responder should avoid direct contact with such fluids whenever possible and use barriers like face shields, masks, or shields designed to protect against splashing.

5. Mental and Emotional Safety

While physical protection is paramount, responders should also be aware of their mental and emotional well-being. Emergencies can be stressful, and it is important for BLS providers to remain calm and focused. Emotional protection can involve mental preparedness, ensuring that the responder is not overwhelmed by the situation and is able to perform necessary actions without compromising their safety. Additionally, it is important to communicate effectively with bystanders or team members to ensure that the situation is managed as safely as possible.

6. Ensuring the Safety of Others

While assessing scene safety and personal protection, it is important to consider the safety of bystanders as well. If others are around, including family members or witnesses, their well-being should also be ensured. In some cases, they may be able to assist, but in others, they may need to be moved away from the danger zone or provided with instructions on how to help.

Assessing scene safety and ensuring personal protection are critical first steps in any emergency situation. The responder must be vigilant, quickly evaluating potential hazards and taking the necessary precautions to prevent injury or exposure. By prioritizing safety for themselves and others, BLS providers can confidently deliver care, knowing that they have minimized risks while improving the chances of a successful intervention. A quick, calm, and informed assessment of scene safety can ultimately save lives and protect responders from harm.

SECTION IV

Key Equipment for BLS Providers

Key equipment for Basic Life Support (BLS) providers is essential for performing the core interventions needed in life-threatening emergencies, particularly cardiac arrest, respiratory distress, and choking. Having the right tools at hand and knowing how to use them properly can significantly improve patient outcomes. Below is a comprehensive explanation of the key equipment that BLS providers rely on to perform their duties effectively.

1. Automated External Defibrillator (AED)

An Automated External Defibrillator (AED) is a portable device that can assess a person's heart rhythm and deliver an electric shock (defibrillation) if needed to restore a normal heart rhythm. AEDs are used in cases of sudden cardiac arrest caused by rhythms like ventricular fibrillation (VF) or pulseless ventricular tachycardia (VT). These devices are designed to be user-friendly, with voice prompts and visual instructions guiding the user through the process. For BLS providers, the ability to quickly access and use an AED is crucial, as early defibrillation significantly increases the chances of survival. AEDs are widely available in public spaces and should be used immediately following the initiation of high-quality chest compressions if the person is unresponsive and not breathing normally.

2. Rescue Breathing Barriers

A rescue breathing barrier is an important piece of equipment for providing artificial ventilation when someone's breathing has stopped or is insufficient. It is typically a mask or face shield that creates a barrier between the provider and the patient during mouth-to-mouth resuscitation, thereby reducing the risk of disease transmission. Rescue breathing barriers often feature a one-way valve that ensures air flows only from the provider to the patient and not in reverse. These barriers are critical for protecting the BLS provider and delivering effective breaths without the risk of cross-contamination.

3. Gloves

Disposable gloves are essential for protecting both the BLS provider and the patient from exposure to bodily fluids, such as blood or saliva, that may be encountered during resuscitation efforts. Gloves also provide a level of hygiene and prevent contamination when performing chest compressions, mouth-to-mouth resuscitation, or managing wounds. BLS providers are encouraged to carry gloves in their emergency kits to ensure their own safety while maintaining the integrity of the care they provide.

4. CPR Manikin

While not typically used in real emergencies, a CPR manikin is an important tool for training BLS providers. These practice dummies simulate real human anatomy and allow individuals to practice chest compressions and rescue breathing. Training with a CPR manikin ensures that BLS providers can effectively perform CPR techniques, including proper hand placement, compression depth, rate, and timing. Manikins are equipped with feedback mechanisms to guide proper technique, which is crucial for developing the muscle memory needed to perform life-saving CPR in high-pressure situations.

5. Oxygen Delivery Equipment

For advanced BLS providers, oxygen delivery equipment, such as bag-valve masks (BVM) or oxygen tanks, may be necessary for patients who are not breathing or whose breathing is inadequate. The BVM is a manual resuscitation device that provides positive pressure ventilation to a patient who is not breathing on their own. It consists of a self-expanding bag, a unidirectional valve, and a face mask. Oxygen tanks are used to supply supplemental oxygen, particularly for patients who are in respiratory distress. BLS providers should be familiar with using these devices effectively to ensure proper ventilation and oxygenation, which are critical for brain and organ function.

6. Suction Devices

Suction devices are used to clear the airway of any obstructions, such as vomit, blood, or secretions, which can block the patient's ability to breathe. Effective airway management is a core component of BLS, and removing any debris from the airway can help prevent suffocation and allow for better ventilation during resuscitation efforts. Portable suction devices are available and are often used in more advanced BLS settings, particularly in ambulances or in hospitals.

7. Airway Adjuncts

Airway adjuncts are tools used to maintain or open the airway in patients who are unconscious or semi-conscious. Two common types of airway adjuncts used in BLS are the oropharyngeal airway (OPA) and nasopharyngeal airway (NPA). The OPA is a rigid device inserted into the mouth to prevent the tongue from blocking the airway, while the NPA is a softer tube inserted through the nose. These adjuncts help to keep the airway open while providing ventilation, especially in patients who are not fully conscious and unable to protect their own airway.

8. Trauma Shears

Trauma shears are essential for emergency situations where clothing, seat belts, or other materials may need to be cut away to gain access to the patient. These shears are designed with a blunt tip for safe cutting around the patient's body, especially in critical areas such as the chest or abdomen. BLS providers use trauma shears to quickly expose the patient's chest or limbs for interventions like CPR or defibrillation, making it a key tool in emergency care.

9. First Aid Kit

A basic first aid kit is important for addressing minor injuries and managing bleeding, burns, or other injuries that may occur in the aftermath of a medical emergency. A standard first aid kit typically includes items like bandages, antiseptic wipes, gauze pads, adhesive tape, and other supplies that can help stabilize a patient until more advanced care is available. While the primary focus of BLS is resuscitation, the first aid kit ensures that BLS providers can address secondary injuries or conditions that may arise during the emergency response.

10. Personal Protective Equipment (PPE)

In addition to gloves, BLS providers may also carry other forms of personal protective equipment (PPE), such as face shields, masks, and gowns. These are particularly important in situations where there is a risk of bloodborne or airborne pathogens. PPE helps protect the provider from potential exposure to infectious diseases while also ensuring that the resuscitation efforts are conducted safely and effectively.

Each piece of equipment serves a specific purpose and is designed to ensure that BLS providers can deliver high-quality, life-saving interventions. Having access to the right tools, knowing how to use them efficiently, and practicing proper technique are all essential components of effective Basic Life Support. Whether performing CPR, using an AED, or managing an airway, BLS providers are equipped with the necessary tools to stabilize a patient and enhance their chances of survival.

EXERCISE I

1. What is the primary goal of Basic Life Support (BLS)?

2. What is the first thing a rescuer should do upon arriving at the scene of an emergency?

3. Why is it important to assess scene safety before initiating care?

4. What is the correct way to check for responsiveness in an unconscious adult?

5. How long should a rescuer spend checking for normal breathing and a pulse?

6. What should the rescuer do if the patient is unresponsive and not breathing normally?

7. Why is it important to minimize interruptions during CPR?

8. What are the five links in the Chain of Survival?

9. How does high-quality CPR differ from basic CPR?

10. What personal protective equipment (PPE) is recommended for rescuers during BLS?

11. What is the compression-to-ventilation ratio for a single rescuer performing CPR on an adult?

12. How deep should chest compressions be for an adult during CPR?

13. At what rate should chest compressions be performed?

14. Why is full chest recoil important during CPR?

15. What is the purpose of the head-tilt, chin-lift maneuver?

16. When should an automated external defibrillator (AED) be used?

17. What are the key steps in using an AED?

18. How can rescuers reduce the risk of gastric inflation during rescue breaths?

19. What is the primary purpose of the Chain of Survival?

20. What should rescuers do if they are unsure whether the patient has a pulse?

CHAPTER THREE
Adult Basic Life Support

SECTION I

Step-by-Step Adult BLS Process

The Step-by-Step Adult Basic Life Support (BLS) process outlines the critical actions needed to provide immediate care to a person experiencing a medical emergency, such as sudden cardiac arrest (SCA) or respiratory failure. BLS is essential for sustaining life until advanced medical care is available. Here's a detailed, step-by-step breakdown of the BLS process for adults:

1. Ensure Scene Safety

Before approaching a patient, the first and foremost step is to ensure that the scene is safe. This includes assessing the environment for potential hazards, such as traffic, fire, electrical wires, or any other dangers that could harm the rescuer or the patient. If the scene is unsafe, try to move the patient to a safer location if possible, without putting yourself at unnecessary risk. If the environment is secure, move on to the next step.

2. Check for Responsiveness

Approach the person and gently tap or shake their shoulder while loudly asking, "Are you okay?" You need to determine if the person is responsive. If the individual does not respond to these stimuli, it is an indication of a potential medical emergency. If the person is unresponsive, immediately proceed to activate the emergency response system.

3. Call for Help (Activate EMS)

If the person is unresponsive, immediately call for help or instruct someone nearby to call emergency medical services (EMS), such as dialing 911. When activating EMS, provide clear and concise information, including the patient's location, the nature of the emergency, and the patient's condition. If you are alone and have access to a phone, call EMS first before proceeding with any further steps, especially if you are unsure of the help available in your area.

4. Check for Breathing and Pulse

Once EMS has been alerted, quickly assess the person's breathing and pulse. Place your ear near the person's mouth to listen for any normal breathing sounds and simultaneously observe for chest rise and fall. Simultaneously check for a pulse by placing two fingers on the carotid artery (on the side of the neck, just below the jaw) for no more than 10 seconds. If the person is not breathing or is only gasping and does not have a pulse, this indicates the need for immediate intervention with CPR.

5. Begin Chest Compressions

If the person is not breathing and has no pulse, start CPR with chest compressions. Position your hands in the center of the person's chest, right on the lower half of the breastbone (sternum). Place the heel of one hand on the sternum, and the other hand on top of the first. Interlace your fingers and keep your arms straight, with your shoulders directly over your hands. Perform compressions at a depth of at least 2 inches (5 cm) for an adult, at a rate of 100 to 120 compressions per minute. Allow the chest to fully recoil between compressions, ensuring that the heart and blood vessels receive adequate refilling.

6. Provide Rescue Breathing (if trained)

After 30 chest compressions, if you are trained in giving rescue breaths, proceed with providing two rescue breaths. To perform rescue breaths, first ensure that the person's airway is open by tilting the head back and lifting the chin (the head-tilt, chin-lift maneuver). Pinch the person's nose closed, and create a tight seal over their mouth with yours. Deliver a breath that lasts about one second, ensuring that the chest rises. Give a second breath in the same manner. If you are unable or unwilling to give mouth-to-mouth breaths, continue with chest compressions only (hands-only CPR), which is still effective in many cases.

7. Continue CPR Cycles

Repeat cycles of 30 chest compressions and 2 rescue breaths until one of the following occurs:

- The person begins to show signs of life (such as moving, breathing normally, or responding).
- Emergency medical services (EMS) or a trained responder arrives to take over.
- An automated external defibrillator (AED) is ready to be used.
- You become too exhausted to continue.

8. Use an AED (if available)

As soon as an Automated External Defibrillator (AED) becomes available, turn it on and follow the device's voice prompts. AEDs are designed to be simple and user-friendly, with clear instructions to guide you through the process. Attach the AED pads to the person's bare chest, ensuring that the pads are placed on the upper right chest and the lower left side of the chest, below the rib cage. Once the pads are properly placed, the AED will analyze the person's heart rhythm. If the AED detects a shockable rhythm, it will prompt you to deliver a shock. Stand clear of the patient while the shock is administered. After the shock, immediately resume CPR starting with chest compressions.

9. Continue CPR and Defibrillation

If the person remains unresponsive after the shock, continue performing high-quality CPR, following the same cycle of chest compressions and rescue breaths. If the AED advises another shock, repeat the process until EMS arrives or the person starts showing signs of life. If the AED does not advise a shock, continue CPR and reassess the person's condition every two minutes.

10. Post-Resuscitation Care

Once the person is revived or EMS arrives to take over, provide them with any information about the situation, including how long the person was unresponsive and whether CPR or AED was used. Follow any additional instructions from EMS or healthcare providers to ensure continued care. If the person regains consciousness, monitor their condition closely, provide reassurance, and keep them as calm and comfortable as possible until professional medical help is available.

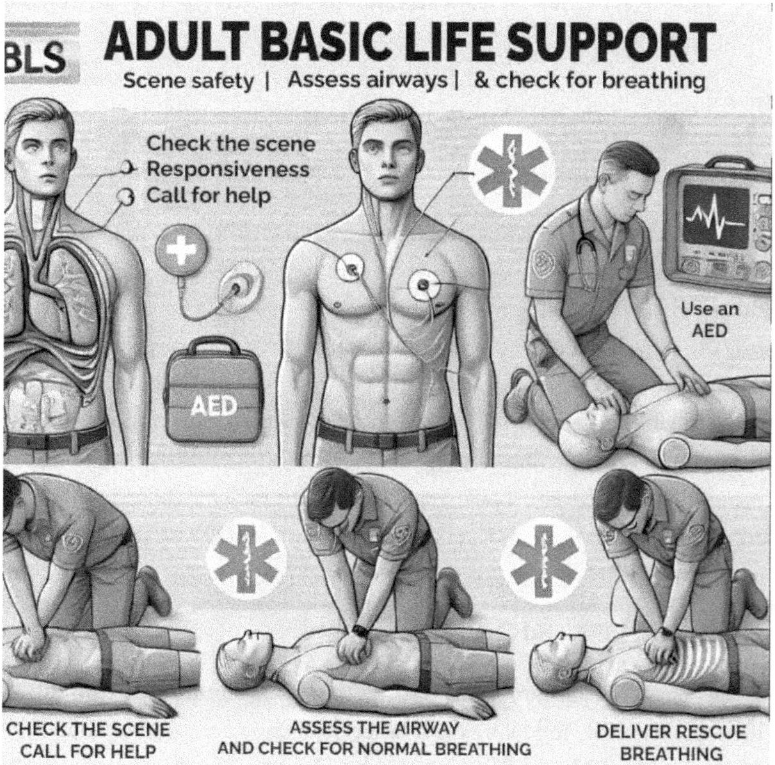

Fig. 2 Adult Basic Life Support (BLS)

Throughout the entire process, it is important to remain calm and focused, following each step methodically. Basic Life Support can save lives, and the prompt, high-quality performance of these steps plays a critical role in improving survival outcomes in cases of sudden cardiac arrest.

SECTION II

High-Quality Chest Compressions

High-quality chest compressions are the foundation of effective cardiopulmonary resuscitation (CPR) and are critical to improving the chances of survival for individuals experiencing sudden cardiac arrest (SCA). When the heart stops beating effectively, as in SCA, chest compressions are essential to maintaining blood flow to vital organs, especially the brain and heart, until more advanced medical care can restore a normal heartbeat. The goal of chest compressions is to simulate the heart's pumping action, keeping oxygenated blood circulating through the body and helping to preserve organ function.

To achieve high-quality chest compressions, several key factors must be followed. First, the depth of the compressions is crucial. Compressions must be deep enough to ensure that the heart is being adequately squeezed to pump blood. For an adult, the depth should be at least 2 inches (5 cm) deep. Compressing the chest too shallowly reduces the effectiveness of the compressions, meaning less blood is circulated to vital organs. On the other hand, compressing the chest too deeply can cause injury to the ribs or internal organs, so maintaining the correct depth is vital.

The rate of chest compressions is also an important factor. The compressions should be performed at a rate of 100 to 120 compressions per minute, which corresponds to the beat of the song "Stayin' Alive" by the Bee Gees. This rate has been shown to be the most effective for maintaining blood flow while minimizing fatigue for the person performing the CPR. Going too slow can reduce the effectiveness of blood circulation, while going too fast may not allow for adequate filling of the heart between compressions.

Another critical component of high-quality chest compressions is allowing full chest recoil between compressions. This means that after each compression, the chest should return to its normal position. If the chest does not recoil fully, it reduces the efficiency of the heart's refilling phase and decreases the overall effectiveness of the compressions. It is important to avoid leaning on the chest between compressions, as this can impede the heart's ability to refill with blood.

Additionally, minimizing interruptions in chest compressions is essential for maintaining continuous blood circulation. Each interruption, such as during pauses for rescue breaths or when checking the pulse, reduces the amount of blood circulating to the brain and other organs. High-quality CPR involves minimizing these pauses and ensuring compressions are continuous for as long as possible. In cases where an automated external defibrillator (AED) is available, it should be used as quickly as possible to minimize interruptions in compressions.

Proper hand placement is also critical to delivering effective chest compressions. The heel of one hand should be placed on the center of the chest, along the lower half of the sternum, with the other hand placed on top to provide additional force. The elbows should be locked, and the body weight should be used to help with the compressions, ensuring enough force is applied to achieve the correct depth without straining the rescuer.

The person performing the compressions should also be prepared for the physical demands of delivering high-quality CPR. It requires strength and endurance, so it's important to switch with another rescuer every 2 minutes if possible to avoid fatigue, which can reduce the effectiveness of compressions.

In conclusion, high-quality chest compressions are essential to the success of CPR and can significantly improve a patient's chance of survival following sudden cardiac arrest. They should be deep enough, fast enough, and allow for complete chest recoil while minimizing interruptions. By following these principles, CPR providers can deliver the most effective compressions, preserving vital organ function and increasing the likelihood of survival until advanced medical care arrives. Proper training and practice are necessary to ensure that chest compressions are performed correctly and efficiently, making a life-saving difference in critical situations.

SECTION III

Rescue Breathing Techniques for Adults

Rescue breathing is a critical component of cardiopulmonary resuscitation (CPR) when the person is not breathing or breathing inadequately but still has a pulse. For adults, rescue breathing involves providing oxygen to the patient's lungs by breathing into their mouth or nose to help maintain adequate oxygen levels in the body until normal breathing is restored or advanced medical help arrives. Proper rescue breathing can prevent brain damage and other organ dysfunction by ensuring that oxygen continues to circulate in the bloodstream.

In adult CPR, rescue breathing is typically performed when the patient is unresponsive and has no normal breathing (or abnormal, gasping breaths). When initiating rescue breathing, it's important to follow the correct technique to ensure that the air reaches the lungs effectively without causing harm.

The *first* step in performing rescue breathing is to ensure the patient's airway is open. This is done by tilting the head backward and lifting the chin, which helps to clear the airway. In an unconscious adult, the tongue can obstruct the airway, so the head-tilt, chin-lift maneuver is necessary to open it. It is important to keep the airway open throughout the process to ensure the air reaches the lungs.

Next, the rescuer should pinch the patient's nose shut and take a deep breath. The rescuer then places their mouth over the patient's mouth, forming a tight seal to prevent air from escaping. The rescuer should then exhale steadily and gently into the patient's mouth, watching for the chest to rise. This indicates that air is entering the lungs. A full breath should be delivered in about 1 second, ensuring that the chest rises adequately but not excessively. The aim is to provide enough air to fill the lungs without overinflating them, which can cause damage or reduce the effectiveness of the breathing.

After one full breath, the rescuer should pause and watch for the patient's chest to fall, indicating that the air is being exhaled. The rescuer should continue to provide rescue breaths in a cycle, giving two breaths after every 30 chest compressions, if performing full CPR. This ratio is commonly referred to as "*30:2*," which means ***30 chest compressions followed by 2 rescue breaths.***

It is important to avoid over-ventilating the patient, which can lead to complications such as gastric inflation, where air enters the stomach instead of the lungs. This can lead to choking or vomiting, which could further complicate the situation. To avoid this, each breath should be slow and controlled, ensuring that the patient's chest rises gently and adequately.

If the rescuer is unable to provide rescue breaths due to a lack of training or other factors, hands-only CPR (chest compressions only) should be performed until professional help arrives. However, it is always preferable to provide rescue breaths if the rescuer is trained and able to do so effectively, as it ensures that the body's oxygen supply is maintained until further medical intervention is available.

One additional consideration in rescue breathing is the use of a barrier device, such as a pocket mask or a bag-valve mask (BVM), which provides a safer way to deliver breaths without direct contact with the patient's mouth. A barrier device reduces the risk of transmitting infectious diseases and can also create a better seal for more effective ventilation. In a healthcare setting, or for those with higher levels of training, using such devices is often recommended.

Rescue breathing for adults should continue until one of the following occurs: the patient begins to breathe normally on their own, emergency medical personnel arrive and take over, or the rescuer becomes exhausted and is unable to continue. It is essential to keep the airway open and maintain proper ventilation for as long as possible to maximize the chances of survival.

Rescue breathing is a vital skill in CPR that helps provide oxygen to an unresponsive adult patient who is not breathing or is breathing inadequately. The technique involves opening the airway, delivering controlled breaths that cause the chest to rise, and continuing the cycle of breaths and chest compressions. By following proper technique, rescuers can maintain adequate oxygen levels in the patient's bloodstream, minimizing the risk of brain damage and improving the likelihood of recovery. Proper training in rescue breathing is essential for anyone who might be called upon to assist in a life-threatening emergency.

SECTION IV

Hands-Only CPR

Hands-Only CPR is a simplified version of traditional cardiopulmonary resuscitation (CPR) that focuses solely on high-quality chest compressions without the need for mouth-to-mouth resuscitation. This technique has been recommended for use by bystanders in cases of sudden cardiac arrest (SCA), especially in situations where the rescuer may feel uncomfortable or untrained in delivering rescue breaths. Hands-Only CPR has been shown to be an effective and life-saving method for sustaining circulation until more advanced medical help arrives or until the patient regains spontaneous circulation.

The main principle behind Hands-Only CPR is that chest compressions alone can provide sufficient blood flow to vital organs, particularly the brain and heart, during cardiac arrest. While traditional CPR involves both chest compressions and rescue breaths, research has shown that for adults in sudden cardiac arrest, chest compressions alone are just as effective as full CPR in maintaining circulation. The key benefit of Hands-Only CPR is that it eliminates the need for mouth-to-mouth ventilation, which some people may find challenging, uncomfortable, or hesitant to perform. By focusing on compressions only, it encourages more people to act in emergency situations, increasing the likelihood that bystanders will intervene.

To perform Hands-Only CPR correctly, it is important to follow a few simple but critical steps. The first step is to assess the situation and determine if the person is unresponsive and not breathing normally. If the person is unresponsive and not breathing, immediately call emergency services (911 or the local emergency number) to activate the EMS system.

It's important to remember that early activation of EMS is critical to ensuring the best chances of survival.

Once EMS has been called, the next step is to begin high-quality chest compressions. To do this, place the heel of one hand on the center of the person's chest, along the lower half of the sternum, and place your other hand on top of the first. With your arms straight and elbows locked, use your upper body weight to push down firmly and quickly, compressing the chest at least 2 inches (5 cm) deep. The compressions should be performed at a rate of 100 to 120 compressions per minute, roughly the same speed as the beat of the song "Stayin' Alive" by the Bee Gees. It is essential to allow the chest to fully recoil between compressions, as this helps the heart refill with blood and improves the effectiveness of the compressions.

The main difference between Hands-Only CPR and traditional CPR is that there is no need to perform rescue breathing. In traditional CPR, mouth-to-mouth breaths are given to provide oxygen to the person's lungs, but in Hands-Only CPR, the focus remains solely on compressions. Oxygen in the blood that remains in the body following cardiac arrest is typically sufficient for a short period, allowing high-quality chest compressions to maintain circulation to the heart and brain. By continuing compressions without interruption, the body can maintain enough blood flow to vital organs until professional medical help arrives or an automated external defibrillator (AED) is used.

While Hands-Only CPR is effective for most adults who experience sudden cardiac arrest, it is not recommended for children, infants, or individuals who have experienced cardiac arrest due to drowning or respiratory causes. In these cases, traditional CPR, which includes both chest compressions and rescue breaths, is recommended. However, for adults experiencing SCA due to a sudden heart problem, Hands-Only CPR provides a simple, effective, and immediate way to help.

One of the main advantages of Hands-Only CPR is that it is easy to learn and perform, even for individuals with no formal CPR training. Many organizations, including the American Heart Association (AHA), have promoted Hands-Only CPR as a way to encourage more bystanders to take action in emergency situations. Studies have shown that bystanders who perform Hands-Only CPR are more likely to initiate life-saving interventions and are less likely to hesitate due to concerns about performing rescue breaths. The simplicity and ease of this technique have contributed to increased public awareness and confidence in providing aid during cardiac emergencies.

Hands-Only CPR is a life-saving intervention that anyone can perform in an emergency situation to help a person experiencing sudden cardiac arrest. By focusing solely on chest compressions, Hands-Only CPR is effective, easy to learn, and can be performed quickly and efficiently. It removes the barrier of mouth-to-mouth resuscitation, encouraging more people to act when someone is in need of help. By performing high-quality chest compressions at the correct depth and rate, bystanders can increase the chances of survival and provide critical assistance until professional medical responders arrive. Hands-Only CPR is an essential skill that everyone can learn and use to make a difference in an emergency.

EXERCISE II

1. What is the first step in Adult BLS when approaching an unresponsive person?

a) Begin chest compressions

b) Check for breathing and pulse

c) Activate EMS and get an AED

d) Assess the scene for safety

2. What is the correct compression-to-ventilation ratio for a single rescuer performing adult CPR?

a) 15:2

b) 30:2

c) 20:2

d) 10:2

3. What is the recommended chest compression depth for adults during CPR?

a) At least 1 inch

b) 1.5 inches

c) At least 2 inches

d) More than 3 inches

4. What is the correct rate for chest compressions in adult CPR?

a) 80-100 compressions per minute

b) 100-120 compressions per minute

c) 120-140 compressions per minute

d) 60-80 compressions per minute

5. Which part of the hand should be used to perform chest compressions?

a) The fingers

b) The palm of the hand

c) The heel of the hand

d) The knuckles

6. How often should rescuers switch roles during CPR to avoid fatigue?

a) Every 1 minute

b) Every 2 minutes

c) Every 5 minutes

d) Every 10 minutes

7. What should you do immediately after delivering a shock with an AED?

a) Wait for the AED to analyze the rhythm again

b) Check for a pulse

c) Begin chest compressions

d) Deliver rescue breaths

8. What is the primary purpose of chest compressions in CPR?

a) Restart the heart

b) Maintain blood flow to vital organs

c) Provide oxygen to the lungs

d) Clear the airway

9. What should you do if the patient is gasping but has no pulse?

a) Provide rescue breaths only

b) Perform CPR immediately

c) Wait for the AED to arrive

d) Roll the patient into the recovery position

10. How can you minimize interruptions during chest compressions?

a) Perform quick pulse checks every 5 compressions

b) Prepare the AED while compressions continue

c) Stop compressions during AED pad placement

d) Switch rescuers after every compression cycle

11. What is the recommended action if the chest does not rise during rescue breaths?

a) Stop CPR immediately

b) Reposition the airway and try again

c) Deliver 5 back blows

d) Increase the force of the breath

12. Where should AED pads be placed on an adult?

a) Both pads on the upper chest

b) One pad on the lower left chest and the other on the upper right chest

c) Both pads on the lower abdomen

d) One pad on the sternum and the other on the back

13. How do you ensure effective chest compressions?

a) Compress as fast as possible

b) Maintain proper depth and rate with full chest recoil

c) Lean on the chest between compressions

d) Use only one hand for compressions

14. What is the purpose of the "head-tilt, chin-lift" technique?

a) To deliver more effective chest compressions

b) To maintain an open airway

c) To increase blood flow to the brain

d) To ensure a better AED shock

15. What is the first thing you should do when an AED arrives at the scene?

a) Turn it on

b) Place the pads on the chest

c) Perform another pulse check

d) Deliver a shock

16. What action should be taken if a bystander is performing poor-quality chest compressions?

a) Let them continue to avoid confusion

b) Take over and provide high-quality compressions

c) Wait for EMS to arrive

d) Correct them but let them continue

17. What should you do if the AED advises "No shock needed"?

a) Perform another pulse check

b) Resume chest compressions immediately

c) Turn off the AED

d) Begin rescue breaths only

18. Which of the following is a sign of effective chest compressions?

a) The rescuer's hands remain stiff

b) The chest rises during compressions

c) The patient's skin turns pale

d) The chest recoils fully after each compression

19. What is the recommended duration for each rescue breath in adult CPR?

a) 0.5 seconds

b) 1 second

c) 2 seconds

d) 3 seconds

20. What is the most reliable indicator of ROSC (Return of Spontaneous Circulation)?

a) Gasping for air

b) Pupillary response

c) A palpable pulse

d) A sudden jerking motion

CHAPTER FOUR
Pediatric Basic Life Support

SECTION I

Recognizing Pediatric Arrest

Recognizing pediatric arrest is a crucial skill for anyone involved in emergency care, especially for those providing Basic Life Support (BLS). Pediatric cardiac arrest can be caused by a variety of factors, including respiratory failure, trauma, drowning, or a severe allergic reaction. Since children's bodies and responses to emergencies differ significantly from adults, it is vital to recognize signs of pediatric arrest early in order to initiate timely interventions and improve survival outcomes.

1. Signs of Respiratory Distress or Arrest

Unlike adults, cardiac arrest in children is often preceded by respiratory distress or failure. This means that if a child shows signs of struggling to breathe or becomes unresponsive after difficulty breathing, the arrest may be imminent. Key signs of respiratory distress include rapid or labored breathing, flaring nostrils, grunting, or wheezing. If these signs are not addressed promptly, they can progress to respiratory arrest, where the child stops breathing completely.

2. Unresponsiveness and Lack of Normal Breathing

The most prominent indicator of pediatric cardiac arrest is unresponsiveness combined with the absence of normal breathing. A child in cardiac arrest will typically become unresponsive, meaning they will not respond to verbal or physical stimulation. In cases of pediatric arrest, it is important to check for signs of normal breathing. Normal breathing includes regular, even breaths. Gasping, irregular breathing, or complete cessation of breath indicates a serious emergency. If the child is unresponsive and not breathing normally, this is a clear sign of arrest.

3. Pulse Check

In pediatric patients, it is crucial to check for a pulse, though doing so can sometimes be challenging, especially in infants or younger children. For infants, the brachial pulse (located on the inside of the upper arm) is checked, while for older children, the carotid pulse (located in the neck) is used. If there is no pulse or if it is extremely weak or slow, the child is likely in cardiac arrest. The absence of a pulse for more than 10 seconds in a child is a critical emergency requiring immediate action.

4. Witnessed vs. Unwitnessed Arrest

Recognizing pediatric arrest is often easier when it is witnessed. In a witnessed arrest, the child may suddenly collapse or stop responding after a traumatic event or sudden medical condition. In an unwitnessed arrest, such as in the case of a child found unresponsive, the signs may be less obvious. It is important to carefully assess the child's breathing and responsiveness before initiating CPR.

5. Preceding Events or Medical History

Children who are at higher risk for sudden cardiac arrest often display certain warning signs or have medical histories that predispose them to arrest. Conditions like congenital heart defects, arrhythmias, asthma, severe infections, or allergic reactions can make children more vulnerable to cardiac or respiratory arrest. Being aware of these risk factors is important for timely recognition. For example, a child with asthma may experience severe difficulty breathing before progressing to respiratory or cardiac arrest.

6. Secondary Signs to Watch For

Other signs that might indicate the onset of pediatric arrest or imminent arrest include a sudden drop in blood pressure, extreme fatigue, or a change in skin color. Cyanosis, or a bluish tint around the lips and face, is a common sign of oxygen deprivation and may indicate that the child is nearing respiratory failure. If the child shows signs of significant distress, such as confusion, dizziness, or an inability to stay awake, this could also be a signal of serious cardiovascular or respiratory compromise.

7. Rapid Assessment and Response

When recognizing pediatric arrest, time is of the essence. An essential aspect of recognizing arrest is being able to differentiate between normal unconsciousness (such as sleeping) and true unresponsiveness due to a life-threatening event. A quick but thorough assessment should include checking the child's responsiveness, breathing, and pulse. If the child is unresponsive and not breathing or has abnormal breathing, it is essential to call emergency services immediately and begin CPR.

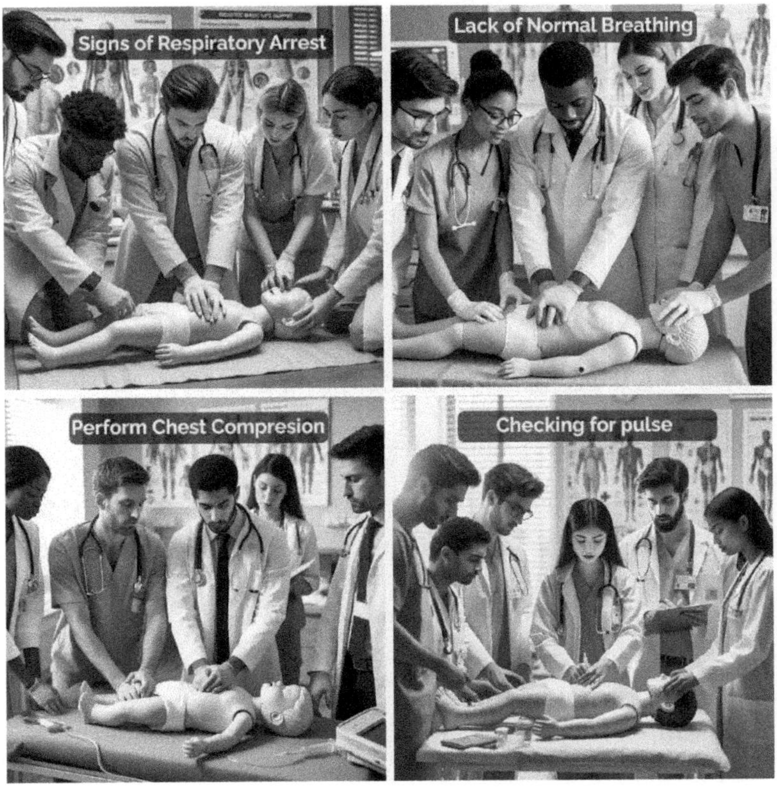

Fig 3. Pediatric Basic Life Support

Recognizing pediatric arrest is different from adult arrest because the majority of pediatric cardiac arrests are due to respiratory problems or as a result of a traumatic event. Therefore, it is important for caregivers, parents, and healthcare providers to be alert to early signs of distress in children. Early recognition and prompt action, including performing high-quality CPR, can greatly improve a child's chances of survival. Understanding the signs and knowing what to do in these critical moments can make a life-saving difference.

SECTION II

Child and Infant CPR Techniques

Child and infant CPR techniques are adapted to the unique anatomical and physiological differences between children, infants, and adults. These variations require modified approaches to ensure the most effective resuscitation efforts. The following explanation outlines the specific techniques for performing CPR on children and infants, with a focus on the differences in hand placement, compression depth, and the use of rescue breaths.

Infant CPR (For children under 1 year of age)

1. Assess the Scene and Check for Responsiveness

Before beginning CPR, assess the scene to ensure it is safe, and then check if the infant is responsive by tapping or gently shaking the baby and calling their name. If the infant does not respond, shout for help and activate emergency medical services (EMS) if possible.

2. Positioning for Chest Compressions

For infants, CPR is performed using two fingers to deliver chest compressions. Place the infant on their back on a firm surface. Use your index and middle fingers placed just below the nipple line on the center of the chest. The depth of the compression should be about 1.5 inches (4 cm), which is roughly one-third of the infant's chest depth. Press down at a rate of 100 to 120 compressions per minute, ensuring that each compression is firm and allows for full recoil.

3. Rescue Breaths

After every 30 chest compressions, give 2 rescue breaths. To provide a proper breath, cover the infant's nose and mouth with your mouth, creating a seal, and gently breathe into the infant's airway. Each breath should last about 1 second and should make the chest rise visibly. Be cautious not to over-inflate the infant's lungs, as this can lead to airway injury.

4. Reassess the Infant's Condition

After 5 sets of 30 chest compressions and 2 breaths, reassess the infant's condition. If the infant shows signs of life or begins breathing normally, turn the baby onto their side to help keep the airway open and continue to monitor them. If the infant remains unresponsive and does not begin breathing, continue CPR until help arrives.

Child CPR (For children aged 1 year to puberty)

1. Assess the Scene and Check for Responsiveness

As with infant CPR, the first step is to assess the scene for safety and check the child's responsiveness by tapping the child gently and shouting their name. If there is no response and the child is not breathing or is only gasping, call for emergency medical help and activate EMS.

2. Positioning for Chest Compressions

For children, chest compressions should be delivered with one or two hands, depending on the size of the child. For smaller children, use one hand, placing it on the center of the chest, just below the nipple line. For larger children or those approaching puberty, you can use both hands, similar to adult CPR. Compressions should be about 2 inches (5 cm) deep, or approximately one-third the depth of the chest, with a compression rate of 100 to 120 per minute. Allow the chest to fully recoil between compressions to maintain effective circulation.

3. Rescue Breaths

After every 30 chest compressions, deliver 2 rescue breaths. To provide a breath, cover the child's nose and mouth with your mouth, ensuring a tight seal. Each breath should take about 1 second, enough to make the child's chest rise visibly. Be careful not to over-inflate the chest, as this could lead to complications like gastric inflation.

4. Reassess the Child's Condition

After 5 cycles (30 compressions and 2 breaths), reassess the child's condition. If the child begins breathing normally or shows signs of life, turn them into the recovery position and continue monitoring. If the child remains unresponsive and does not start breathing, continue CPR until advanced help arrives.

Key Differences Between Infant and Child CPR

- Hand Placement: For infants, chest compressions are performed with two fingers, whereas for children, one or two hands are used depending on the size of the child.
- Compression Depth: Infant compressions should be about 1.5 inches (4 cm), while child compressions should be about 2 inches (5 cm).
- Rescue Breaths: The technique for rescue breaths remains the same for both infants and children, but it's important to adjust the strength of the breaths according to the size of the patient. For infants, gentle breaths are required to avoid over-inflating the lungs, while children can typically tolerate slightly stronger breaths.

In both child and infant CPR, minimizing interruptions to chest compressions is key. Effective CPR involves ensuring that each compression is deep and performed at the correct rate, while also delivering rescue breaths with appropriate volume and timing. If an AED is available and the child is older than 1 year, it should be used according to the manufacturer's guidelines.

When to Seek Professional Help

In any instance where the child or infant does not respond to CPR, it is important to continue with the life-saving measures until emergency responders arrive or the patient begins to show signs of life. Timely CPR and early defibrillation, if needed, are critical components of the Chain of Survival, and immediate action can make a significant difference in the child's or infant's chances of survival.

In summary, while child and infant CPR share many similarities with adult CPR, the key differences lie in the techniques used to account for the smaller size and different physiological needs of these populations. Understanding these distinctions ensures that CPR is performed as effectively as possible, maximizing the chances of survival in a critical emergency.

SECTION III

Compression Depth and Rate for Pediatrics

Compression depth and rate are two of the most critical factors in delivering effective cardiopulmonary resuscitation (CPR) for pediatric patients. While the general principles of CPR remain consistent—ensuring proper blood circulation and oxygen delivery to vital organs until further medical care arrives—pediatric CPR requires specific adjustments to accommodate the smaller size, developing anatomy, and physiological differences of children and infants. These differences necessitate modifications in compression depth, rate, hand placement, and overall technique to minimize the risk of injury while maximizing the chances of survival.

Compression Depth for Infants and Children

The appropriate compression depth is crucial in ensuring that blood is pumped effectively through the body, particularly to the brain and heart, which are most vulnerable during a cardiac arrest.

For **infants** (under 1 year of age), the compression depth should be approximately 1.5 inches (4 cm) or one-third of the depth of the chest. The heart in an infant is relatively small and less resilient than that of an older child or adult, so compressions must be gentle enough to avoid causing rib fractures or damage to the internal organs while still being deep enough to generate effective blood circulation. Given the infant's small size, it is also essential that compressions be performed with care and attention to technique, particularly because their chest is softer and more flexible than that of an older child.

For **children** (aged 1 to puberty), the depth should be at least 2 inches (5 cm) or approximately one-third of the chest depth, as opposed to the deeper compressions required for adults. Since children have more developed bones and structures than infants, compressions can be deeper and more forceful, but excessive pressure should still be avoided. While deeper compressions are required compared to infants, caution is still necessary to prevent the possibility of rib fractures or damage to the chest wall.

Compression depth for both infants and children is carefully calibrated to balance the risk of injury with the need for effective blood flow. If compressions are too shallow, inadequate blood circulation will result, and the chance of survival decreases significantly. Conversely, compressions that are too deep may cause unnecessary injury, particularly to the ribs, internal organs, or heart, and may also cause cardiac arrest in severe cases.

Compression Rate for Infants and Children

The compression rate is another essential factor in pediatric CPR. For both **infants** and **children**, the compression rate should be *100 to 120 compressions per minute*, the same as the rate for adults. This range has been shown to optimize blood circulation, which is critical in maintaining the oxygen supply to vital organs while resuscitation efforts are underway.

The 100-120 compressions per minute rate corresponds to about two compressions per second, and is fast enough to circulate blood effectively but slow enough to allow for full chest recoil between compressions. This rate has been studied and found to be optimal for sustaining blood flow while reducing the likelihood of rescuers tiring too quickly. Chest compressions that are too slow may not effectively circulate blood to vital organs, while compressions that are too fast may not allow enough time for the heart to refill with blood, reducing their effectiveness.

For both **infants** and **children**, it is important to maintain a consistent rhythm, which can be challenging for some rescuers. The "Stayin' Alive" song by the Bee Gees is often used as a rhythm guide, as it has the right tempo for optimal compression rates. This simple mnemonic helps maintain consistency, reducing the likelihood of slowing down or speeding up due to stress or uncertainty.

Hand Placement for Pediatric CPR

Hand placement for chest compressions is another crucial aspect that varies depending on the child's size and age.

For ***infants***, chest compressions should be performed using the two-finger technique. The rescuer should place their two fingers (index and middle) on the center of the infant's chest, just below the nipple line, on the sternum. This method ensures that the compressions are both controlled and gentle, reducing the likelihood of injury to the fragile ribcage and internal organs. It also helps to concentrate the force applied to the chest in a manner that maximizes effectiveness while minimizing risk.

For ***children***, the technique shifts to using either the *heel of one hand* or the *heel of both hands*, depending on the child's size. The heel of one hand should be placed on the lower half of the sternum, and the other hand should be placed on top for added force in larger children. For smaller children, the use of one hand is often enough. For larger children or those who are nearing adolescence, both hands may be needed to generate the force required for adequate compression depth. In either case, it is critical that the rescuer's arms remain straight and that their shoulders are positioned directly over their hands to maximize the force applied to the chest.

In both cases, hand placement should focus on the lower half of the sternum, avoiding the xiphoid process (the small, cartilage-like extension at the bottom of the sternum), which could cause internal injury if compressed.

Full Chest Recoil and Minimizing Interruptions

Full chest recoil is just as important as the depth and rate of compressions. After each compression, the chest must return fully to its normal position before the next compression is applied. This is important because, during recoil, the heart refills with blood, preparing for the next compression. If the chest does not fully recoil, the effectiveness of the compressions is compromised, and the heart cannot refill properly. This is true for all ages, but especially important in pediatric CPR where the heart's ability to fill is more easily hindered by incomplete chest recoil.

In pediatric CPR, minimizing interruptions is crucial. Interruptions should be kept as brief as possible, particularly when switching between rescuers or administering rescue breaths. For infants and children, every interruption or pause in compressions reduces the amount of blood circulated through the body, decreasing the likelihood of survival. Compressions should be continuous and only briefly interrupted for actions like providing rescue breaths or using an AED.

Rescue Breaths and Compression-to-Ventilation Ratio

For **infants and children**, the compression-to-ventilation ratio differs from adults in some situations. When performing CPR on an infant or child, the ratio is typically *30:2* when a single rescuer is performing the CPR. This means that for every 30 chest compressions, two rescue breaths should be given. If two rescuers are present, the ratio changes to *15:2*, which allows for more frequent breaths and better oxygenation of the patient. The technique for delivering these rescue breaths also differs slightly for pediatric patients. For infants, gentle breaths should be given to ensure the chest rises, while for children, the breaths should be delivered with enough force to expand the chest, but not so forcefully that air enters the stomach instead of the lungs.

Compression depth and rate for pediatric CPR are critical factors in ensuring blood is effectively circulated to vital organs and that the patient has the best chance of survival. For infants, compressions should be approximately 1.5 inches (4 cm) deep, and for children, about 2 inches (5 cm) deep. The compression rate should be between 100 and 120 compressions per minute, and compressions should be delivered with minimal interruptions, using proper hand placement to ensure maximum efficiency and minimal risk of injury. By following these guidelines, caregivers and healthcare providers can deliver high-quality CPR that provides the best possible chance for survival in pediatric cardiac arrest situations.

SECTION IV

Special Considerations for Pediatric BLS

Special considerations for pediatric Basic Life Support (BLS) are essential due to the unique physiological and anatomical differences between children and adults. Pediatric patients, including infants (under 1 year) and children (from 1 year to puberty), require modified approaches in BLS to maximize their chances of survival and reduce the risk of injury. Understanding these distinctions is critical for any responder trained in BLS, as improper technique or failure to recognize specific needs can lead to less effective resuscitation.

One of the primary differences in pediatric BLS is the most common cause of cardiac arrest. Unlike adults, where cardiac arrest often results from heart-related issues, pediatric cardiac arrest is usually due to respiratory problems or shock. Therefore, prompt attention to the child's airway and breathing is essential. In cases of respiratory distress or failure, pediatric patients may benefit greatly from rescue breathing before the heart actually stops. Recognizing signs of respiratory compromise, such as increased effort in breathing or cyanosis, is key to intervening early and potentially preventing cardiac arrest.

In terms of technique, chest compressions for infants and children differ from those for adults in both depth and hand placement. For infants, compressions should be about 1.5 inches (4 cm) deep, and a two-finger technique is typically used. The fingers are placed on the breastbone just below the nipple line, while the other hand supports the infant's head to keep the airway open. For children over 1 year, compressions should be about 2 inches (5 cm) deep, and either one or two hands can be used depending on the size of the child and the rescuer's comfort level. This hand placement and depth ensure adequate force is applied without causing injury to the chest wall, which is more delicate in young patients.

The ratio of compressions to breaths is also tailored to pediatric BLS. For children and infants, the recommended compression-to-ventilation ratio when performing BLS alone is 30:2, meaning 30 compressions followed by 2 rescue breaths. However, if two rescuers are available, the ratio changes to 15:2 to allow more frequent breaths, as pediatric cardiac arrests often stem from respiratory issues. Delivering effective rescue breaths is critical, as children are more susceptible to hypoxia. Breaths should be delivered gently to avoid over-inflation, which could lead to air in the stomach (gastric inflation) and possible vomiting.

Airway management in pediatric BLS also requires specific adjustments. Children's airways are more flexible and prone to obstruction, so maintaining an open airway with proper positioning is important. For infants, the head should be in a neutral position to keep the airway clear, while for older children, a slight head tilt-chin lift can help open the airway. Care should be taken not to tilt the head too far, as this can actually close off a child's airway. In cases of suspected trauma, the jaw-thrust maneuver is recommended to avoid neck movement.

Another consideration in pediatric BLS is the use of Automated External Defibrillators (AEDs). AEDs are safe and effective for use in children over the age of 1, but pediatric electrode pads, which deliver a reduced shock dose, are recommended for young children. For infants under 1 year, AED use is less common, but if no other option is available, an AED can be used with extreme caution, and adult pads should be placed so that one pad is on the chest and the other on the back to avoid contact between the pads. Pediatric-specific pads or settings help avoid delivering too high a dose of electrical shock, which can be harmful to smaller bodies.

For infants and children who are choking, BLS protocols also differ. In infants, back slaps and chest thrusts are recommended instead of the abdominal thrusts typically used in adults. Five back slaps, delivered forcefully between the infant's shoulder blades, are alternated with five chest thrusts until the object is dislodged or the infant becomes unresponsive. In older children, abdominal thrusts can be used, but care should be taken not to apply excessive force, as the abdominal organs are more vulnerable to injury in children.

Finally, emotional considerations are important in pediatric BLS. Children may be scared or anxious, and keeping the child calm can improve cooperation and make interventions more effective. Responders should speak gently, explaining actions if possible, and involve the child's parent or caregiver if they are present. For the parents, witnessing their child in distress is traumatic, so clear communication and compassion are critical.

Pediatric BLS requires a specialized approach that accounts for physiological and emotional differences from adult BLS. Adjustments in technique, depth, rate of compressions, and breathing ratio ensure that children and infants receive the most appropriate care for their size and developmental needs. Proper training and awareness of these special considerations empower BLS providers to deliver effective, compassionate, and safe interventions in life-threatening situations involving young patients.

EXERCISE III

1. What is the recommended compression depth for children during CPR?

A) At least 1 inch

B) At least 2 inches

C) Approximately one-third the depth of the chest

D) Exactly 3 inches

2. What is the compression-to-ventilation ratio for single-rescuer CPR in children?

A) 15:2

B) 30:2

C) 20:2

D) 10:2

3. For two-rescuer pediatric CPR, what is the correct compression-to-ventilation ratio?

A) 15:2

B) 30:2

C) 20:2

D) 10:2

4. When performing CPR on an infant, where should you place your hands?

A) One hand on the forehead and two fingers on the center of the chest

B) Two thumbs encircling the chest with fingers supporting the back

C) Both hands on the center of the chest

D) Two fingers on the lower half of the sternum

5. How often should rescuers switch roles during two-rescuer CPR to avoid fatigue?

A) Every 1 minute

B) Every 2 minutes

C) Every 3 minutes

D) Every 5 minutes

6. What is the recommended rate of compressions for pediatric CPR?

A) 60-80 compressions per minute

B) 80-100 compressions per minute

C) 100-120 compressions per minute

D) 140-160 compressions per minute

7. How should you open an infant's airway?

A) Neutral position with head tilt and chin lift

B) Full head tilt

C) No head movement; compress the chest

D) Hyperextend the neck

8. What is the recommended ventilation rate for a child with a pulse but no normal breathing?

A) 10-12 breaths per minute

B) 12-20 breaths per minute

C) 6-8 breaths per minute

D) 20-24 breaths per minute

9. What is the first step in using an AED on a child?

A) Turn on the AED

B) Check the child's breathing

C) Place the pads on the chest

D) Deliver a shock immediately

10. Where should AED pads be placed on a child?

A) Both pads on the chest, side by side

B) One pad on the chest and one on the back

C) Both pads on the back

D) One pad on the left side of the chest and one on the stomach

11. For infants, what is the correct compression technique during two-rescuer CPR?

A) One-hand chest compressions

B) Two-thumb encircling hands technique

C) Two-finger technique

D) Two-hand chest compressions

12. How long should you check for a pulse in an unresponsive child?

A) No more than 5 seconds

B) No more than 10 seconds

C) No more than 15 seconds

D) No more than 20 seconds

13. What is the preferred location to check the pulse in an infant?

A) Radial artery

B) Carotid artery

C) Femoral artery

D) Brachial artery

14. In pediatric BLS, when should you begin CPR?

A) If the child is unresponsive and breathing normally

B) If the child is unresponsive and not breathing or only gasping

C) If the child is responsive but has an irregular heartbeat

D) If the child has a pulse but is not breathing normally

15. What is the maximum time you should pause compressions to deliver breaths?

A) 5 seconds

B) 10 seconds

C) 15 seconds

D) 20 seconds

16. How should you respond if an infant has a foreign body airway obstruction and becomes unresponsive?

A) Deliver back blows only

B) Perform chest compressions immediately and check the mouth for the object

C) Begin abdominal thrusts

D) Perform rescue breathing immediately

17. What is the ideal hand position for performing chest compressions on a child?

A) Lower half of the sternum

B) Upper half of the sternum

C) Center of the chest, directly over the xiphoid process

D) Over the ribcage

18. What should you do if a child's pulse is less than 60 beats per minute and they have poor perfusion despite adequate ventilation?

A) Only provide rescue breaths

B) Start chest compressions

C) Administer defibrillation

D) Wait for advanced care

19. How many back slaps should you deliver to a choking infant before chest thrusts?

A) 3 back slaps

B) 5 back slaps

C) 10 back slaps

D) Continuous back slaps until the object is expelled

20. What is the most common cause of cardiac arrest in children?

A) Congenital heart defects

B) Respiratory failure or shock

C) Trauma

D) Drug overdose

CHAPTER FIVE

Automated External Defibrillator (AED) Use

SECTION I

Understanding AED Functionality

An Automated External Defibrillator (AED) is a portable, user-friendly medical device designed to help restore a normal heart rhythm in cases of sudden cardiac arrest (SCA). AEDs are critical tools in the Chain of Survival, as they enable rapid defibrillation, significantly increasing the chances of survival for individuals in cardiac arrest. Understanding AED functionality is essential for anyone who might be involved in a cardiac emergency.

1. Purpose of an AED

An AED delivers an electric shock to the heart, which can correct certain types of abnormal heart rhythms, such as ventricular fibrillation (VF) and pulseless ventricular tachycardia (VT). These rhythms occur when the heart's electrical system malfunctions, causing the heart to quiver or beat abnormally fast rather than pumping blood effectively. The AED's shock aims to "reset" the heart, allowing it to return to a normal rhythm and resume proper blood flow.

2. Components of an AED

An AED typically includes the following components:

- Electrodes (Pads): The adhesive pads are placed on the patient's chest to deliver the electric shock and monitor the heart's rhythm.

- Analyzing System: This system detects and analyzes the heart's electrical activity to determine if a shock is needed.
- Battery: Powers the device, allowing it to be used in various locations without needing an external power source.
- Audio and Visual Prompts: AEDs guide users with clear, step-by-step voice instructions, and some models may also have visual indicators or screens.

3. Steps for Using an AED

Step 1: Turn on the AED

Most AEDs activate automatically when the lid is opened, but if not, there will be a power button. Once on, the AED will provide voice instructions guiding the user through each step.

Step 2: Attach the Electrodes

- Placement of Pads: Place one pad on the upper right side of the chest, just below the collarbone, and the other pad on the lower left side, about a hand's width below the armpit.
- Ensure Proper Contact: The electrodes must have good contact with the skin, so remove any clothing, wipe away moisture, and, if necessary, shave the chest area to ensure the pads adhere well.

Step 3: Allow the AED to Analyze

Once the pads are attached, the AED will automatically analyze the heart rhythm. It's essential that no one touches the patient during this time, as movement can interfere with the analysis. The AED will announce, "Analyzing heart rhythm; do not touch the patient."

Step 4: Deliver the Shock if Advised

- Shock Button: If a shock is advised, the AED will instruct the user to press a button to deliver it. Some AEDs are fully automated and will deliver the shock automatically after a countdown.

- Clear the Patient: Before pressing the shock button, ensure that everyone is clear of the patient by saying "Clear!" This avoids accidental injury to bystanders.
- Shock Delivery: The AED will deliver an electric shock that travels through the pads to the heart, which may momentarily stop the heart's abnormal rhythm, allowing it to reset.

Step 5: Continue CPR if Needed

After delivering the shock, the AED will typically prompt the user to resume CPR if no normal rhythm is detected. Continue chest compressions and follow the AED's prompts. The AED will automatically reanalyze the heart rhythm every 2 minutes, guiding you through additional shocks or CPR as necessary until emergency medical services arrive.

4. Safety Considerations

- Avoid Wet Surfaces: Do not use an AED on a patient lying in water, as this could lead to electrical injury. Move the patient to a dry area if possible.
- Clear Metal Objects: Remove any metal objects, such as jewelry, that may interfere with pad placement. However, do not delay AED use for minor adjustments.
- Avoid Contact During Shock Delivery: Make sure everyone stands clear of the patient before delivering a shock to prevent accidental electrical injury.

5. Maintenance and Accessibility of AEDs

- Battery Checks: AEDs should be checked regularly to ensure the battery is functional and ready for emergency use.
- Pad Replacement: Electrodes are typically single-use and must be replaced after each use or after expiration.
- Placement in Public Areas: AEDs should be installed in easily accessible locations in public spaces, workplaces, and other high-traffic areas. Clear signage and visibility increase the likelihood of AED use during an emergency.

6. Importance of Training and Familiarity

Although AEDs are designed to be user-friendly, training on how to use an AED can improve response time and confidence during an emergency. Basic Life Support (BLS) training often includes AED usage, preparing individuals to recognize when defibrillation is needed and perform CPR effectively alongside AED use.

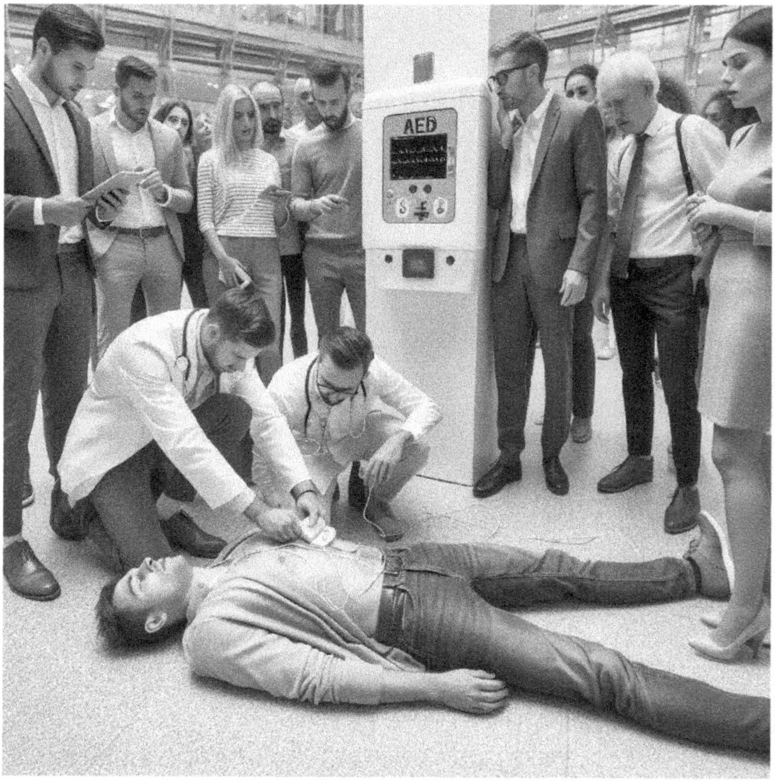

Fig. 4 Automated External Defibrillator use on patient

AEDs play a crucial role in resuscitation by providing immediate defibrillation, which is often essential for the survival of cardiac arrest victims. Understanding the AED's functionality and following the device's prompts carefully can make a life-saving difference. Regular maintenance and public accessibility further enhance the effectiveness of AEDs, empowering both trained responders and bystanders to act confidently in emergencies.

SECTION II

Applying AED in Cardiac Arrest Scenarios

Applying an Automated External Defibrillator (AED) in cardiac arrest scenarios is a crucial, life-saving intervention that can restore a person's heart rhythm in cases of sudden cardiac arrest (SCA). Cardiac arrest typically occurs due to a malfunction in the heart's electrical system, which leads to irregular, ineffective heart rhythms such as ventricular fibrillation (VF) or pulseless ventricular tachycardia (VT). Both conditions prevent the heart from pumping blood, quickly depriving the brain and vital organs of oxygen. Without intervention, brain cells begin to die within minutes, and the chance of survival decreases by approximately 10% for each minute without defibrillation. The AED is designed to reverse these rhythms, giving victims of cardiac arrest the best chance of survival when combined with high-quality CPR.

When cardiac arrest is identified—signaled by the victim being unresponsive and not breathing or only gasping—immediate action is necessary. First, ensure that emergency services have been called, then retrieve an AED if available or have someone bring it to the scene. Turning on the AED is the first and often simplest step; AEDs are designed to be intuitive, guiding responders with clear visual instructions and verbal prompts. Many devices activate automatically when the lid is opened, making it straightforward for even untrained bystanders to initiate use.

The next critical step is pad placement, which must be precise to ensure effective delivery of the electric shock. AED pads are adhesive and come with diagrams or clear labels indicating their correct positioning. For adults, the first pad should be placed on the upper right chest, just below the collarbone, and the second pad on the lower left side of the chest, a few inches below the armpit. This placement creates a pathway through the heart, allowing the electrical shock to travel across the heart muscle and “reset” the heart’s electrical system. Pediatric cardiac arrest cases, though less common, require special considerations. Pediatric AED pads, designed to deliver a lower energy shock, should be used for children under eight years old or weighing less than 55 pounds; if unavailable, adult pads can be used, with placement adjusted so they do not touch each other. For infants, one pad is placed in the center of the chest and the other in the center of the back, ensuring effective current flow through the heart.

Once the pads are attached, the AED will begin to analyze the heart’s rhythm automatically or prompt the responder to initiate the analysis. During this analysis, no one should touch the patient, as any movement or contact can interfere with the AED’s ability to accurately assess the heart rhythm. AEDs are programmed to deliver a shock only when a shockable rhythm—such as VF or pulseless VT—is detected. This feature prevents unnecessary shocks, as non-shockable rhythms, such as asystole or pulseless electrical activity (PEA), require different medical interventions. If a shockable rhythm is detected, the AED will prompt the responder to press a “Shock” button to deliver the shock. Some AEDs, particularly in professional healthcare settings, are fully automatic and will deliver the shock without additional action from the responder.

When the AED delivers a shock, it sends a brief but high-energy pulse of electricity across the heart muscle. This “stuns” the heart, interrupting the abnormal rhythm and giving the heart’s natural pacemaker cells a chance to re-establish a normal rhythm. It is essential for all bystanders and responders to stay clear of the patient during shock delivery to avoid the risk of accidental shock to others and to ensure that the full electrical dose is delivered solely to the patient.

Following shock delivery, or if no shock is advised, the AED will prompt the responder to resume CPR immediately. Effective CPR, with minimal interruptions, is vital as it maintains blood circulation, delivering oxygen to the brain and organs until a normal heart rhythm can be restored. AEDs are typically programmed to re-evaluate the heart’s rhythm every two minutes, allowing for a continuous cycle of CPR and AED analysis. If the AED advises a second shock after two minutes of CPR, the cycle will repeat, with CPR and shocks continuing until emergency medical personnel arrive or the patient begins to show signs of recovery, such as spontaneous breathing or movement.

Effective teamwork during AED application can enhance the success of resuscitation efforts. In scenarios with multiple responders, one person can manage chest compressions while another operates the AED, minimizing the time between compressions and shocks. Efficient coordination and clear communication—such as confirming when the AED is analyzing or when the shock is about to be delivered—ensure that CPR is continuous and that safety protocols are followed during defibrillation.

AED use in cardiac arrest situations requires attention to safety and practical considerations. For instance, if the victim has a wet chest (such as in cases of drowning), the chest should be dried to ensure the pads adhere properly and to reduce the risk of electrical arcing during defibrillation. If the patient is lying in a puddle or is wet, move them to a dry area if feasible before applying the AED. In cases where the person has a lot of chest hair, it may be necessary to shave the area where the pads will be placed, as excessive hair can reduce the pads' contact with the skin, diminishing the effectiveness of the shock. Additionally, if the patient has an implanted medical device, such as a pacemaker or defibrillator, place the pads at least one inch away from it to avoid interference.

The availability of AEDs in public spaces, such as airports, malls, schools, and sports arenas, has dramatically improved the survival rates for out-of-hospital cardiac arrest. Many AEDs are strategically placed in these areas, often in marked, accessible locations, to allow immediate access in emergencies. The simplicity of AEDs, combined with their widespread availability, makes it possible for bystanders to deliver early defibrillation, an intervention shown to double or even triple the chances of survival when applied promptly after cardiac arrest.

Therefore, applying an AED in cardiac arrest scenarios involves a series of structured steps: recognizing cardiac arrest, turning on the AED, placing the pads correctly, staying clear during rhythm analysis, delivering a shock if advised, and resuming CPR promptly. Following these steps ensures that the responder can deliver potentially life-saving care. Training in AED use is a valuable skill, as familiarity with the device and confidence in applying it can reduce hesitation and improve outcomes in real-life emergencies. This combination of CPR and AED intervention provides the highest possible chance for a successful resuscitation and significantly improves survival rates in cardiac emergencies.

SECTION III

Steps for Safe and Effective AED Use

Using an Automated External Defibrillator (AED) can significantly improve the chances of survival for a person experiencing sudden cardiac arrest. AEDs are designed to be user-friendly and can be operated by anyone with basic training in CPR and AED use.

The following steps outline the correct and safe way to use an AED effectively in an emergency:

1. Ensure Scene Safety

Before approaching the victim, check the surroundings to make sure the scene is safe for you and any bystanders. Look for hazards, such as traffic, fire, water, or any other potentially dangerous conditions. Only proceed if it's safe to do so.

2. Assess the Victim and Call for Help

Confirm that the victim is unresponsive and not breathing normally. If the person is not breathing or only gasping, instruct someone nearby to call emergency services (911 or the local emergency number) and bring the AED. If you are alone, make the call yourself and retrieve the AED if it's within reach.

3. Turn on the AED

Once the AED arrives, turn it on immediately by pressing the power button or opening the lid, depending on the model. The AED will start giving verbal and visual instructions to guide you through the process.

4. Expose the Victim's Chest and Attach the Pads

Quickly expose the victim's chest by removing or cutting away any clothing. If the chest is wet, dry it off, as moisture can interfere with the electrical current. Open the electrode pads package, and peel off the backing to reveal the sticky side. Place one pad on the upper right side of the chest, just below the collarbone, and the other pad on the lower left side, below the armpit. Most AED pads have illustrations showing the correct placement.

5. Ensure Everyone is Clear of the Victim

Once the pads are in place, the AED will analyze the victim's heart rhythm. Make sure no one, including yourself, is touching the victim during this analysis. Say, "Clear!" out loud and visually check that everyone is clear before allowing the AED to proceed with the analysis.

6. Allow the AED to Analyze and Follow Prompts

The AED will automatically analyze the heart rhythm and determine if a shock is necessary. If a shock is advised, the AED will instruct you to press the "shock" button. Ensure that everyone is still clear of the victim before pressing the button to deliver the shock. Some AEDs are fully automated and will deliver the shock without requiring you to press a button, so continue to follow the prompts closely.

7. Deliver the Shock if Advised

If a shock is advised, press the "shock" button, ensuring everyone is still clear. The AED will administer the shock, which aims to reset the heart's rhythm. After the shock is delivered, the AED will prompt you to begin CPR immediately if the victim is still unresponsive.

8. Resume CPR Immediately

After delivering a shock, or if no shock is advised, immediately begin CPR starting with chest compressions. Continue following the AED's prompts, as it will instruct you when to pause CPR for additional rhythm analysis.

Perform high-quality chest compressions at a rate of 100–120 per minute and a depth of at least 2 inches for adults.

9. Continue Following AED Instructions Until EMS Arrives

Keep performing CPR and follow the AED's prompts until emergency medical services (EMS) personnel arrive and take over or until the victim shows signs of regaining consciousness, such as breathing normally or moving. The AED will continue to analyze the heart rhythm periodically and will instruct you if an additional shock is needed.

10. Do Not Turn Off the AED

Leave the AED on and attached to the victim until EMS arrives, as it may be needed again. The AED's data can also be used by EMS professionals to assess the victim's condition.

Using an AED effectively involves staying calm, following the instructions carefully, and ensuring the safety of everyone involved. The AED is a life-saving device that, when used correctly, can help restore a normal heart rhythm and dramatically improve a victim's chances of survival in sudden cardiac arrest situations. Practicing AED use as part of CPR training can help prepare you to respond quickly and confidently in real emergencies.

SECTION IV

Troubleshooting Common AED Issues

Troubleshooting common issues with an Automated External Defibrillator (AED) is essential for ensuring the device functions properly during a cardiac emergency. AEDs are designed to be user-friendly, but issues can arise that may prevent the device from delivering a shock or completing the analysis process. Understanding how to troubleshoot these problems can make a significant difference in a critical situation.

Here is a guide to troubleshooting common AED issues:

1. AED Will Not Power On

If the AED does not turn on, first check the battery. Many AEDs have a battery status indicator, but if this is not visible or accessible, try replacing the battery if possible. Regularly scheduled maintenance and battery checks can prevent this issue. In public places, AEDs should be inspected routinely to ensure batteries are fully charged and ready for use. If the AED still doesn't power on after battery replacement, it may have an internal malfunction, and an alternative AED should be used if available.

2. Pads Are Not Adhering to the Patient's Chest

AED pads need to make good contact with the patient's skin to deliver a shock effectively. If the pads do not stick, it could be due to excessive moisture, chest hair, or the presence of oils or lotions on the skin. Dry the patient's chest if it is wet, and shave any excessive chest hair if a razor is available, as some AEDs include a razor for this purpose. Make sure to place the pads on a clean, dry surface for optimal adhesion. Expired or damaged pads may also lose their stickiness, so replace them with new pads if available.

3. AED Delivers a "Check Pads" or "Check Electrodes" Message

The AED may prompt "Check Pads" or "Check Electrodes" if it is not detecting a secure connection with the pads. Reconfirm that the pads are fully adhered to the patient's chest and that the cable connecting the pads to the AED is firmly plugged in. Some AEDs have detachable cables that can become loose, so ensure the connection is secure. If the message persists, try using a new set of pads, as the current set may be defective.

4. AED Will Not Analyze the Heart Rhythm

An AED may fail to analyze the heart rhythm if there is too much motion or interference. Make sure no one is touching the patient, as this can disrupt the AED's ability to read the heart rhythm. Movement from the environment, such as a bumpy surface, can also cause problems; if possible, place the patient on a stable surface. Additionally, certain electromagnetic devices nearby, like cell phones, can interfere with analysis, so keep such items away from the AED.

5. AED Says "No Shock Advised" When the Patient Has No Pulse

AEDs are designed to detect specific shockable heart rhythms, such as ventricular fibrillation or pulseless ventricular tachycardia. In cases of asystole (a flatline) or pulseless electrical activity (PEA), the AED will not advise a shock. This message can be confusing but is an indication to continue CPR, as defibrillation is not effective in these situations. Continue high-quality chest compressions and follow the AED's prompts to reanalyze periodically.

6. AED Indicates a Low Battery During Use

If the AED shows a low battery warning during an emergency, it may still have enough power for a few analyses or shocks, but it is essential to proceed quickly. Deliver the shock if possible, then continue CPR as directed. Regular maintenance checks can prevent this issue, as AEDs should always have a fully charged battery available for use. If the battery fully depletes, replace it if a spare is available, or consider using another AED if one is accessible nearby.

7. Error Messages or Beeping Sounds from the AED

Some AEDs will emit beeping sounds or display error messages if there is an internal malfunction or another operational issue. If this occurs, first try restarting the AED, as some errors can be resolved this way. If the error message continues, and there is no solution in the AED's manual, switch to a backup AED if one is accessible. Some error messages can indicate device issues that require professional maintenance or replacement.

8. AED Does Not Automatically Proceed to Shock Mode

Most AEDs are programmed to analyze and deliver a shock automatically, but if an AED fails to proceed, it could indicate an issue with the device or improper pad placement. Ensure the pads are correctly placed and that there is no interference. Double-check all connections, and if the AED still does not proceed, follow its prompts to restart the process. In some models, pressing the shock button might be necessary, so consult the specific AED model's instructions.

AED troubleshooting is an important part of ensuring readiness during emergencies. Familiarity with these common issues and their solutions can significantly reduce delays and increase the effectiveness of AED intervention. Regular maintenance checks, training, and following the AED's instructions carefully are key practices that help ensure the device will work effectively in the moments that matter most.

EXERCISE IV

1. What is the primary function of an AED?

A) To restart the heart

B) To detect abnormal heart rhythms and deliver a shock if needed

C) To provide oxygen to the patient

D) To monitor blood pressure

2. Which heart rhythm is most commonly treated with an AED?

A) Normal sinus rhythm

B) Ventricular fibrillation (VF)

C) Bradycardia

D) Asystole

3. What is the first step when using an AED?

A) Attach the pads to the patient's chest

B) Turn on the AED

C) Deliver a shock

D) Perform chest compressions

4. Where should AED pads be placed on an adult patient?

A) On the chest and back

B) On the right chest and left side below the armpit

C) Directly over the heart and the stomach

D) Anywhere on the chest

5. What should you do if the AED advises "No Shock Advised"?

A) Turn off the AED

B) Check for a pulse

C) Immediately resume chest compressions

D) Wait for the AED to analyze again

6. What is the purpose of the AED's voice prompts?

A) To guide the rescuer through each step of the process

B) To alert the patient of the shock

C) To notify EMS of the situation

D) To record the events of the rescue

7. If a patient has a pacemaker, how should AED pads be placed?

A) Directly over the pacemaker

B) At least one inch away from the pacemaker

C) Only on the back

D) On the legs

8. What should you do before delivering a shock with an AED?

A) Ensure no one is touching the patient

B) Perform rescue breaths

C) Administer medication

D) Remove all medical jewelry

9. When using an AED on a child under 8 years old, what should you do?

A) Use adult pads and settings

B) Use pediatric pads and settings

C) Place both adult pads on the chest

D) Do not use the AED

10. If the AED pads overlap on a small child, where should they be placed?

A) Both pads on the chest

B) One pad on the chest and one on the back

C) One pad on the arm and one on the chest

D) Do not use the AED

11. How often does the AED reanalyze the heart rhythm?

A) Every 30 seconds

B) Every 2 minutes

C) Every 5 minutes

D) Continuously

12. What should you do if the patient is lying in water?

A) Use the AED immediately

B) Move the patient to a dry area and dry their chest before using the AED

C) Only perform chest compressions

D) Wait for EMS to arrive

13. What should you do if the patient has a medication patch on their chest?

A) Place the AED pad directly over the patch

B) Remove the patch, wipe the skin, and then place the AED pad

C) Avoid using the AED

D) Place the AED pad on the opposite side

14. Why is it important to avoid touching the patient while the AED is analyzing?

A) It prevents the AED from delivering a shock

B) It could result in inaccurate rhythm analysis

C) It causes the patient discomfort

D) It disrupts CPR

15. When is it appropriate to stop using the AED?

A) After one shock

B) When EMS personnel take over

C) After the patient regains consciousness

D) Both B and C

16. Which of the following can interfere with AED pad adhesion?

A) Sweat or wet skin

B) Body hair

C) Medical patches

D) All of the above

17. What is the recommended action if an AED malfunctions?

A) Continue using it while performing CPR

B) Stop CPR and wait for a replacement AED

C) Switch to manual compressions and follow standard BLS protocols

D) Reset the AED and try again

18. What does the AED analyze?

A) The patient's oxygen levels

B) The electrical activity of the heart

C) The patient's blood pressure

D) The patient's respiratory rate

19. What is the best course of action if an AED advises a shock but the patient appears awake and alert?

A) Deliver the shock

B) Reassess the patient's condition and call for advanced care

C) Turn off the AED

D) Perform chest compressions only

20. How can you ensure the AED is ready for use?

A) Check the battery and pads regularly

B) Perform regular maintenance as per manufacturer's instructions

C) Ensure it is stored in an easily accessible location

D) All of the above

CHAPTER SIX

Choking and Airway Management

SECTION I

Recognizing Airway Obstruction

Recognizing airway obstruction quickly and accurately is essential in emergency situations. An obstructed airway can prevent air from reaching the lungs, leading to oxygen deprivation, unconsciousness, and even death if not addressed promptly.

Here are the key steps to recognizing airway obstruction:

1. Identify the Signs of Partial vs. Complete Airway Obstruction

Airway obstructions can be classified as partial or complete. In a partial obstruction, the airway is partially blocked, allowing some air to pass through. Individuals may still be able to cough, make sounds, or breathe with difficulty. Common signs of partial obstruction include noisy breathing, wheezing, and weak coughing.

In contrast, a complete obstruction means no air is passing through the airway at all. In this case, the person will be unable to cough, speak, or breathe. Often, individuals with a complete obstruction may clutch their throat in the universal choking sign and appear panicked or distressed.

2. Look for Signs of Respiratory Distress

Respiratory distress, or difficulty breathing, is often an early indicator of airway obstruction. People experiencing this may have difficulty breathing and show visible signs of struggle, such as gasping or labored breaths.

Additionally, they may develop cyanosis, which is a bluish discoloration of the skin, lips, or fingernails, resulting from a lack of oxygen in the blood.

3. Observe for Changes in Consciousness

A severe airway obstruction will cause a rapid decline in consciousness if not resolved quickly. As oxygen levels drop, the person may become lightheaded, confused, or disoriented, eventually leading to unconsciousness. If someone suddenly collapses without an apparent cause, airway obstruction should be considered as a potential reason, especially if they were eating or in a high-risk situation for choking.

4. Listen for Abnormal Breathing Sounds

Airway obstructions often produce abnormal breathing sounds. In cases of partial obstruction, a high-pitched sound called stridor may be heard as air struggles to pass through the narrowed airway. Wheezing or gurgling sounds may also be present. In a complete obstruction, however, the individual will be unable to make any sounds due to the total blockage, which is an urgent red flag.

5. Assess the Person's Ability to Speak or Cough

One of the quickest ways to determine the severity of an obstruction is to ask the person if they can speak or cough. If they can cough forcefully or talk, it is likely a partial obstruction, and they should be encouraged to continue coughing to try to clear the airway. If they cannot speak, cough, or make any sound, it indicates a complete obstruction, and immediate intervention is required.

6. Look for the Universal Choking Sign

Many people instinctively place their hands around their neck when choking, signaling distress. This is known as the universal choking sign. This gesture can be a clear indicator of airway obstruction, particularly in public or crowded spaces where it may be difficult to hear or observe other symptoms.

7. Evaluate for Potential Causes of Airway Obstruction

Understanding potential causes of airway obstruction can help in assessing and recognizing the issue. Common causes include choking on food or foreign objects, especially in young children or elderly adults. Swelling of the airway, as seen in allergic reactions (anaphylaxis), infections, or trauma, can also obstruct the airway. In medical settings, obstructions can also occur due to the positioning of the tongue in an unconscious person or foreign objects in the mouth or throat.

8. Monitor for Signs of Airway Obstruction in Children

Children, especially infants and toddlers, are at higher risk for airway obstructions due to their smaller airways and tendency to put objects in their mouths. Signs of airway obstruction in children may include weak or ineffective coughing, gagging, drooling, or a sudden onset of distress while eating or playing. Children may also become suddenly quiet or display a fearful expression, which can indicate difficulty in breathing.

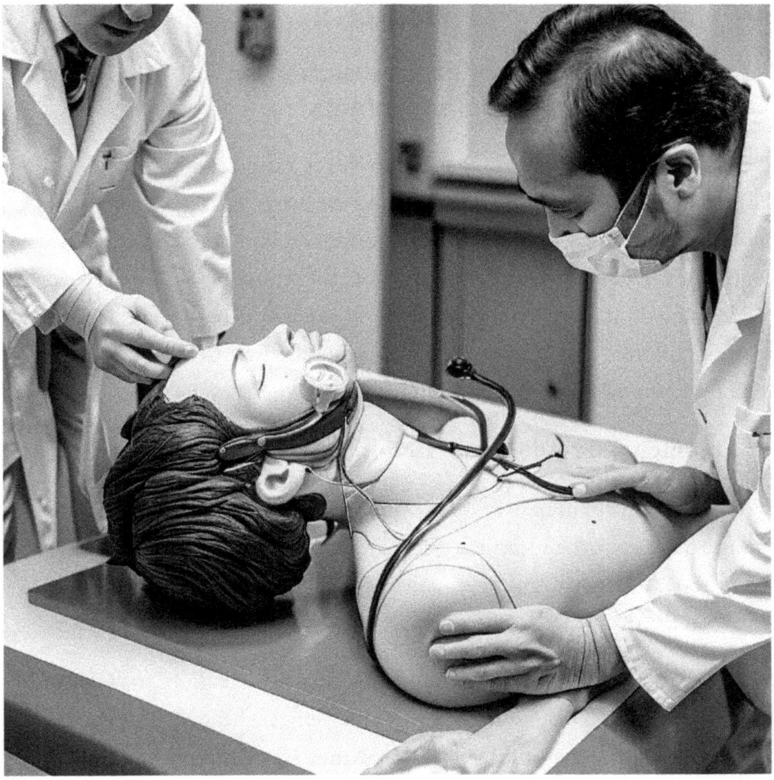

Fig 5. Recognizing Airway Obstruction

Recognizing airway obstruction quickly and accurately is essential for providing the correct response. If an obstruction is suspected, prompt action, such as performing abdominal thrusts (the Heimlich maneuver) for adults and children or back blows and chest thrusts for infants, may be necessary. Knowing how to recognize and respond to airway obstruction can save lives by restoring airflow before more severe consequences occur.

SECTION II

Techniques for Removing Obstructions in Adults, Children, and Infants

When an individual is choking, their airway is partially or completely obstructed, preventing air from reaching the lungs. Removing the obstruction quickly is essential, as prolonged choking can lead to severe injury or even death. The techniques used for removing obstructions differ depending on the age of the patient, as different approaches are needed for adults, children, and infants. Here is a comprehensive explanation of the techniques used for each age group.

1. Techniques for Adults and Children (Ages 1 and Older)

For adults and children over one year of age, the primary technique used to relieve choking is the Heimlich maneuver, or abdominal thrusts. This technique is designed to create an artificial cough, using a forceful upward push on the diaphragm to expel the obstructing object.

- Assess the Situation: If the individual can cough or make sounds, encourage them to continue coughing as this may dislodge the object. Do not intervene unless they are unable to cough or breathe effectively, as interference may push the object further down.
- Stand Behind the Person: For adults and older children, stand behind the choking person and place your arms around their waist. Make sure they are slightly bent forward to avoid forcing the object deeper into the airway.
- Perform Abdominal Thrusts: Make a fist with one hand and place it just above the navel, thumb side in. Grasp your fist with your other hand and deliver quick, forceful upward thrusts into the abdomen. Repeat until the object is expelled or the person becomes unconscious.
- If the Person Becomes Unconscious: Gently lower them to the ground and start CPR if trained, checking the airway for obstructions each time you deliver rescue breaths. Call for

emergency assistance if the obstruction does not clear immediately.

2. Techniques for Pregnant Women and Obese Individuals

For pregnant women or obese individuals, abdominal thrusts may not be effective due to anatomical differences. In these cases, chest thrusts are recommended instead.

- Stand Behind the Person: Position yourself behind the person, as you would for abdominal thrusts.
- Perform Chest Thrusts: Place your arms around the chest rather than the abdomen. Position your hands on the lower half of the sternum, avoiding the xiphoid process to prevent injury. Deliver firm, inward thrusts against the chest.
- Repeat as Necessary: Continue the thrusts until the object is expelled or the person becomes unresponsive, and follow the same procedure for unconsciousness as with the Heimlich maneuver.

3. Techniques for Infants (Under 1 Year of Age)

For infants, abdominal and chest thrusts are too forceful and can cause injury. Instead, back slaps and chest thrusts are used to safely expel the obstruction.

- Position the Infant: Sit down and hold the infant face-down along your forearm, using your thigh for support. Make sure the infant's head is lower than their chest to use gravity to help dislodge the object.
- Perform Back Slaps: Use the heel of your hand to deliver five firm back slaps between the infant's shoulder blades. These slaps should be forceful but controlled, to create enough vibration to dislodge the object without causing harm.
- Turn the Infant Over: If the object does not clear, carefully turn the infant onto their back, using your thigh for support. Ensure that the head remains lower than the chest.
- Perform Chest Thrusts: Using two fingers, deliver five quick chest thrusts on the infant's breastbone, just below the nipple line.

These thrusts should be gentle yet firm, pressing inward and downward.

- Alternate Back Slaps and Chest Thrusts: Continue alternating five back slaps and five chest thrusts until the object is expelled or the infant becomes unresponsive.

4. When the Victim Becomes Unconscious (All Age Groups)

If the choking victim becomes unconscious, different steps should be taken. Here is what to do for adults, children, and infants:

- Lay the Person on a Firm Surface: Gently lower the unconscious person to the ground to prepare for CPR.
- Begin CPR: Start CPR immediately, performing chest compressions. After each set of compressions, open the airway and check for the obstructing object.
- Look for the Object: If you can see the object in the mouth, try to remove it with a finger sweep, but only if it's visible. Do not perform a blind sweep, as this can push the object further down the airway.
- Attempt Rescue Breaths: After checking for the object, deliver two rescue breaths. If the breaths do not go in, resume compressions and continue the cycle until emergency personnel arrive or the object is expelled.

5. Seeking Emergency Medical Assistance

Regardless of age, emergency medical assistance should be sought if the person remains unconscious or if the obstruction cannot be cleared. Even if the object is expelled and the person recovers, medical evaluation is recommended, as complications from the obstruction or the removal process may occur.

In essence, each age group requires specific techniques for effectively clearing airway obstructions. Abdominal thrusts work for most adults and children, while chest thrusts are recommended for pregnant women and obese individuals. For infants, back slaps and chest thrusts are the safest approach. Knowing these techniques and recognizing when to use them can save lives in emergencies involving choking.

SECTION III

Using Advanced Airway Tools

Using Advanced Airway Tools in a medical emergency, particularly during resuscitation efforts like CPR, involves the use of specialized equipment designed to secure and maintain a patient's airway. These tools are used after basic airway management techniques (such as head-tilt chin-lift or jaw-thrust) have been applied and may be necessary in cases where more control or precision is needed to ensure that air can flow freely to the lungs. Advanced airway tools are typically used by healthcare professionals or trained rescuers in settings like hospitals, ambulances, or during other medical emergencies.

1. Endotracheal Tube (ETT)

The endotracheal tube is one of the most commonly used advanced airway tools. It is a flexible tube inserted into the trachea (windpipe) through the mouth or nose to ensure that the airway remains open. The ETT allows for direct ventilation of the lungs and is usually connected to a mechanical ventilator or a bag-valve mask (BVM) for respiratory support. This tool is typically used when a patient is unable to breathe on their own due to obstruction or when other methods of airway management are ineffective.

- Insertion: The tube is inserted via the mouth (or less commonly the nose) while the patient's head is tilted backward to provide a clear passage to the trachea.
- Placement Confirmation: Proper placement is confirmed using methods such as auscultation (listening for breath sounds), capnography (monitoring CO2 levels), or chest rise.
- Indications: Severe airway obstruction, respiratory failure, or inability to maintain an open airway.

2. Laryngeal Mask Airway (LMA)

The LMA is a less invasive alternative to the endotracheal tube and is inserted into the patient's throat to create a seal over the larynx, allowing air to flow into the lungs. It is often used in emergency situations when intubation (endotracheal intubation) is difficult or inappropriate. The LMA does not require advanced skill for insertion and is often used in emergency settings, particularly in cases where a patient's airway is at risk, but intubation is not immediately feasible.

- Insertion: The LMA is placed into the pharynx, with the mask portion sitting over the laryngeal inlet, and it is inflated to form a seal.
- Indications: It is typically used for short-term airway management during resuscitation, anesthesia, or in cases where other airway management tools fail.

3. Combitube (Esophageal Tracheal Tube)

The Combitube is a dual-lumen airway device that can be inserted into the esophagus or the trachea. It is designed for use when more advanced airway management is required, and it is particularly useful in situations where the anatomy is difficult to access, or when other airway tools fail. It can be used in both conscious and unconscious patients.

- Insertion: The tube is inserted into the mouth, and the provider can choose to place it in either the esophagus or the trachea. It has two separate cuffs, one for securing the esophagus and the other for the trachea.
- Indications: Used when intubation or LMA placement is not possible or when there is difficulty in confirming airway placement.

4. King Airway

The King Airway is a supraglottic airway device used to secure the airway in patients who are unresponsive and have no gag reflex. It is inserted through the mouth and provides a secure route for ventilation, particularly when there is difficulty achieving a clear airway using other tools like the LMA or endotracheal tube.

- Insertion: The King Airway is placed into the oropharynx, and once in place, it is inflated to form a seal over the larynx and trachea.
- Indications: It is used for situations where securing an airway is difficult, such as in patients with difficult anatomy or trauma.

5. Supraglottic Airway Devices

Supraglottic airway devices, such as the i-gel and the LMA, are designed to sit above the vocal cords, providing a stable airway that prevents airway collapse or obstruction. These devices are commonly used in situations where endotracheal intubation is not possible or when a quicker insertion is required.

- Insertion: The device is inserted into the mouth or pharynx and forms a seal around the glottis, ensuring airflow to the lungs.
- Indications: These devices are used in emergencies where airway access is needed quickly and effectively, such as during cardiac arrest or trauma.

6. Ventilator Support

Once advanced airway tools are in place, ventilator support may be required to assist the patient's breathing. This can be achieved through mechanical ventilators or bag-valve masks, depending on the tool used for airway management. Proper ventilatory support ensures that the patient is receiving adequate oxygen and ventilation until they can breathe on their own or until they are stabilized for further care.

- Indications: If the patient is unable to breathe or maintain adequate oxygenation on their own, mechanical ventilation or manual ventilation using a bag-valve mask can assist in the process.

7. Monitoring and Maintenance

Once an advanced airway tool is in place, it is crucial to monitor the patient for signs of effective ventilation and to ensure that the airway remains patent (open). This includes watching for chest rise, auscultating for breath sounds, and monitoring vital signs such as oxygen saturation (SpO2) and end-tidal CO2 (ETCO2). Any signs of airway displacement or obstruction should prompt immediate action to reposition or replace the airway device.

- Indications: Continuous monitoring ensures that the patient is receiving proper ventilation and that the airway remains secure throughout the resuscitation process.

The use of advanced airway tools is a vital component of managing critical respiratory and cardiac emergencies. These devices enable healthcare professionals to secure a patient's airway, deliver adequate ventilation, and optimize the chances of survival. Proper training in the use of these tools is essential for effective emergency care, ensuring that each device is used appropriately and safely in accordance with the patient's needs and the clinical situation.

SECTION IV

Airway Management for Non-Breathing Patients

Airway management is a critical component of basic life support (BLS) and involves ensuring that a non-breathing patient's airway is open and clear to allow for effective ventilation. When a person stops breathing or is not breathing adequately, the primary concern is the ability to restore airflow to the lungs, as lack of oxygen can lead to irreversible brain damage or death within minutes. Therefore, airway management is one of the first steps in resuscitating a non-breathing patient, particularly in cases of cardiac arrest, choking, or trauma.

The first step in airway management is to assess the airway. If a person is unresponsive and not breathing, it is important to check for obstructions. Airway obstruction is a common cause of respiratory failure, and it can occur due to the tongue falling back into the throat, foreign objects blocking the airway, or swelling from trauma. The key to effective airway management is ensuring that the airway is open so that oxygen can reach the lungs.

The head-tilt, chin-lift maneuver is typically used to open the airway in an unresponsive, non-breathing patient. This maneuver involves tilting the patient's head backward to lift the chin and open the airway. This action helps to move the tongue away from the back of the throat, which is often the primary cause of airway obstruction in an unconscious patient. For patients with suspected neck injuries, the jaw-thrust maneuver should be used instead. The jaw-thrust maneuver avoids tilting the head and should be performed by lifting the jaw forward while stabilizing the neck. This method is critical in patients with possible cervical spine injuries, as it minimizes movement and reduces the risk of further spinal damage.

Once the airway is open, the next step is to assess the patient's breathing. If the patient is not breathing, or is only gasping, rescue breathing should be initiated. In adults, rescue breathing is typically provided through mouth-to-mouth ventilation. If trained and able, the rescuer should pinch the patient's nose closed, create a tight seal over the patient's mouth with their own, and deliver a breath that lasts about 1 second, making sure the chest rises. This is done for two breaths before continuing with chest compressions. If an adequate seal cannot be made, a face shield or barrier device can be used to deliver breaths more effectively and safely.

For patients who have a persistent airway obstruction due to choking, airway management may involve techniques to clear the obstruction, such as abdominal thrusts (Heimlich maneuver) or back blows and chest thrusts for infants. If the obstruction cannot be cleared using these methods, and the patient remains unresponsive and not breathing, advanced airway management such as the insertion of an advanced airway device (e.g., an endotracheal tube or supraglottic airway) may be required by healthcare providers.

In situations where mouth-to-mouth ventilation is not feasible or the rescuer is not trained in providing rescue breaths, chest compressions alone (hands-only CPR) may be performed. Although this method doesn't directly address the issue of airway obstruction, it helps maintain blood circulation to vital organs until professional help arrives or the patient's breathing is restored.

For advanced airway management, when trained providers arrive on the scene or when more specialized equipment is available, airway devices such as endotracheal tubes or supraglottic airway devices may be inserted to secure the airway and provide more controlled ventilation. These devices ensure that the airway remains open and provide a secure way to deliver oxygen directly to the lungs, bypassing potential blockages or difficulties associated with manual ventilation.

During the course of airway management, it is also important to constantly monitor the patient's airway to ensure that it remains open. For instance, if the patient starts breathing on their own or if they begin to gag or vomit, the airway may become obstructed again and require repositioning or suctioning. Proper suctioning of the airway is vital in clearing any foreign material, such as vomit or blood, to prevent aspiration and improve ventilation.

In cases where advanced airway techniques are not immediately available, the priority should be to focus on providing high-quality chest compressions and attempting to maintain an open airway through the basic maneuvers. It's essential to remember that airway management is not a static process; as the patient's condition evolves, so too should the methods used to maintain the airway, depending on the available resources and level of training of the responder.

In conclusion, airway management for non-breathing patients is a fundamental component of effective resuscitation. Ensuring that the airway is clear and open allows for the delivery of oxygen to the lungs and helps to prevent brain damage and other serious complications. From basic maneuvers like head-tilt, chin-lift to more advanced interventions like endotracheal intubation, the goal is to maintain a clear path for airflow. By following proper airway management protocols, both basic and advanced care providers can significantly improve a patient's chances of survival following a respiratory or cardiac emergency.

EXERCISE V

1. What is the first step to take when you suspect someone is choking?

a. Start chest compressions

b. Perform back blows immediately

c. Ask, "Are you choking?"

d. Call 911 without assessing the situation

2. What does it mean if a choking victim is making high-pitched wheezing sounds?

a. The airway is completely blocked

b. There is a partial airway obstruction

c. They are hyperventilating

d. They are experiencing cardiac arrest

3. What should you do for a conscious adult who is choking and cannot cough?

a. Perform abdominal thrusts (Heimlich maneuver)

b. Start CPR immediately

c. Encourage them to drink water

d. Slap their back until they breathe

4. How should you assist a choking infant who cannot cough, cry, or breathe?

a. Perform abdominal thrusts only

b. Deliver 5 back blows followed by 5 chest thrusts

c. Perform chest compressions immediately

d. Place them in the recovery position

5. When performing abdominal thrusts on a conscious adult, where should your hands be placed?

a. On the victim's chest, just above the sternum

b. On the victim's back, between the shoulder blades

c. Above the navel and below the ribcage

d. Directly on the navel

6. What is the recommended action if a choking victim becomes unconscious?

a. Continue abdominal thrusts until help arrives

b. Begin CPR immediately, starting with chest compressions

c. Place them in the recovery position

d. Wait for EMS to arrive without intervention

7. Which of the following is NOT a sign of severe airway obstruction?

a. Inability to speak or make sounds

b. Coughing forcefully

c. Blue or cyanotic skin

d. Clutching at the throat

8. What is the universal sign for choking?

a. Clutching the stomach

b. Clutching the throat

c. Raising both hands in the air

d. Waving for help

9. How should back blows be delivered to a choking infant?

a. With one hand while holding the infant upright

b. Using firm strikes between the infant's shoulder blades while supporting their head

c. With alternating strikes to the chest and back

d. Gently tapping the infant's back

10. What is the proper body position for delivering chest thrusts to a choking infant?

a. Infant seated in a high chair

b. Infant lying flat on the ground

c. Infant face-up on your forearm, with their head lower than their chest

d. Infant standing upright

11. What is the primary goal when assisting a choking victim?

a. Call for emergency help

b. Encourage the victim to cough up the obstruction

c. Remove the airway obstruction to restore breathing

d. Begin chest compressions immediately

12. When should an object be removed from the mouth of a choking victim?

a. As soon as you see the victim is in distress

b. Only if it is visible and can be easily removed

c. After chest compressions are started

d. Before EMS arrives

13. Which maneuver should be used for a choking pregnant woman or obese person?

a. Chest compressions

b. Abdominal thrusts

c. Back blows

d. Chest thrusts

14. What should you do if a choking victim is coughing forcefully?

a. Perform abdominal thrusts immediately

b. Encourage them to continue coughing

c. Begin CPR to assist their breathing

d. Give back blows to help expel the object

15. What should you do if the airway remains blocked after attempting 5 back blows and 5 abdominal thrusts?

a. Call EMS and continue the sequence

b. Wait for the victim to lose consciousness before continuing

c. Begin CPR without any further attempts at back blows

d. Use an AED to resolve the obstruction

16. What action should be taken for a choking victim who is unresponsive and not breathing?

a. Perform abdominal thrusts until they regain consciousness

b. Begin CPR, including attempts to open the airway and remove the obstruction

c. Place them on their side to improve breathing

d. Perform rescue breaths only

17. How should you position a choking infant for back blows?

a. Upright in a seated position

b. Face-up on a flat surface

c. Face-down on your forearm, with the head lower than the chest

d. Held vertically by their arms

18. Which of the following is a critical sign that an object has been successfully dislodged?

a. The victim continues to gasp for air

b. The victim begins breathing normally and talking

c. The victim loses consciousness

d. The victim becomes more agitated

19. What is the first step to take if a choking victim becomes unconscious while receiving abdominal thrusts?

a. Place them in the recovery position

b. Perform a blind finger sweep to remove the obstruction

c. Lower them to the ground and begin CPR

d. Continue with abdominal thrusts

20. What is the most effective way to prevent choking emergencies?

a. Encourage eating quickly and talking while eating

b. Avoid performing the Heimlich maneuver unnecessarily

c. Educate individuals about proper chewing and safe swallowing habits

d. Always provide liquids during meals

CHAPTER SEVEN

Special Situations and Modifications in BLS

SECTION I

BLS Modifications for Trauma Victims

Basic Life Support (BLS) modifications for trauma victims involve adjusting standard CPR procedures to accommodate the specific needs and conditions of patients who have sustained physical injuries. Trauma cases, such as those involving severe bleeding, fractures, or head and spinal injuries, require careful consideration to ensure that life-saving techniques are both effective and do not cause further harm. Trauma victims often present with unique challenges that necessitate modifications to traditional BLS practices, particularly in how chest compressions, airway management, and other techniques are performed.

1. Assessing the Scene and Ensuring Safety

Before beginning any BLS intervention on a trauma victim, the first priority is to assess the scene for safety. This includes checking for potential hazards that may pose a threat to the responder or the victim. In trauma situations, there may be risks such as fire, unstable structures, or moving vehicles. It is essential to stabilize the victim while ensuring that the environment is safe to provide care.

2. Assessing the Airway and Cervical Spine Protection

For trauma victims, especially those who may have sustained head, neck, or spinal injuries, airway management requires extra caution. One of the main concerns in trauma cases is preventing further injury to the cervical spine. In cases where spinal injury is suspected, rescuers should avoid excessive movement of the head and neck. When opening the airway, a modified technique called the "jaw-thrust maneuver" should be used instead of the traditional head-tilt, chin-lift method. The jaw-thrust maneuver involves lifting the jaw forward without tilting the head, which helps to open the airway while minimizing the risk of aggravating any cervical spine injury.

3. Chest Compressions in Trauma Victims

For trauma victims who have sustained significant injury to the chest or abdomen, rescuers should avoid direct pressure on areas that may have fractures, internal bleeding, or organ damage. In cases where trauma to the chest is suspected, chest compressions should be performed as close to the center of the chest as possible, while avoiding broken ribs or any visibly injured areas. If a rib fracture is suspected, rescuers should still continue with chest compressions, but they should focus on providing firm, deep compressions that are necessary to circulate blood to vital organs, while being mindful of minimizing any further injury to the chest.

4. Managing Severe Bleeding

Severe bleeding is a common concern in trauma situations and must be controlled before or during CPR. In cases of life-threatening bleeding, such as from a severed artery or open wound, direct pressure should be applied to the wound using a clean cloth or dressing. If the bleeding cannot be controlled with pressure, it may be necessary to use a tourniquet or hemostatic agents (if available) to stop the bleeding. While managing severe bleeding, it is important to keep providing chest compressions, as controlling blood loss and maintaining circulation are both critical.

5. Handling Head and Neck Injuries

In trauma victims with head and neck injuries, special attention must be paid to how the victim is moved. If CPR is needed, it is crucial to minimize any movement of the spine, especially in cases of suspected spinal cord injury. For these patients, manual stabilization of the head and neck should be performed, where the rescuer places their hands on both sides of the victim's head to stabilize the cervical spine. This minimizes the risk of additional injury when performing chest compressions or administering rescue breaths.

6. Special Considerations for Multiple Trauma Victims

In cases where the victim has sustained multiple injuries, such as fractures, internal bleeding, and head trauma, it is important to focus on the most life-threatening injuries first. For example, if the patient is in respiratory or cardiac arrest, CPR and airway management should take precedence over other concerns. However, once the victim is stabilized and the immediate life-threatening injuries are addressed, efforts should be made to prevent further harm by managing other trauma-related conditions.

7. CPR Modifications in Pregnancy

Pregnant trauma victims may also require specific BLS modifications. For women in the second or third trimester of pregnancy, it may be necessary to manually displace the uterus to the left side to alleviate pressure on the inferior vena cava, which can reduce blood return to the heart. This modification helps ensure that adequate blood flow is maintained during chest compressions. If the pregnant woman is in cardiac arrest, rescuers should continue with CPR and, if necessary, initiate defibrillation, as appropriate.

8. Use of an AED in Trauma Situations

In trauma victims, the use of an Automated External Defibrillator (AED) may be indicated if the victim experiences cardiac arrest with a shockable rhythm (e.g., ventricular fibrillation or pulseless ventricular tachycardia). However, if the trauma victim has severe chest injuries, such as broken ribs or a collapsed lung, rescuers should ensure the AED pads are placed properly to avoid injury. As always, it's important to follow the AED prompts and use the device without delay to maximize survival chances.

9. When to Stop Resuscitation Efforts

In some cases, trauma victims may have injuries that are incompatible with life, such as massive head trauma or severe internal bleeding. In these situations, resuscitation efforts should continue until the arrival of emergency medical services or until signs of life are confirmed. If the trauma victim is not responsive to CPR, advanced care may be required, but some cases may not be survivable despite the best efforts of responders. Ethical considerations must also be taken into account, especially in cases where the injuries are so severe that the chances of recovery are negligible.

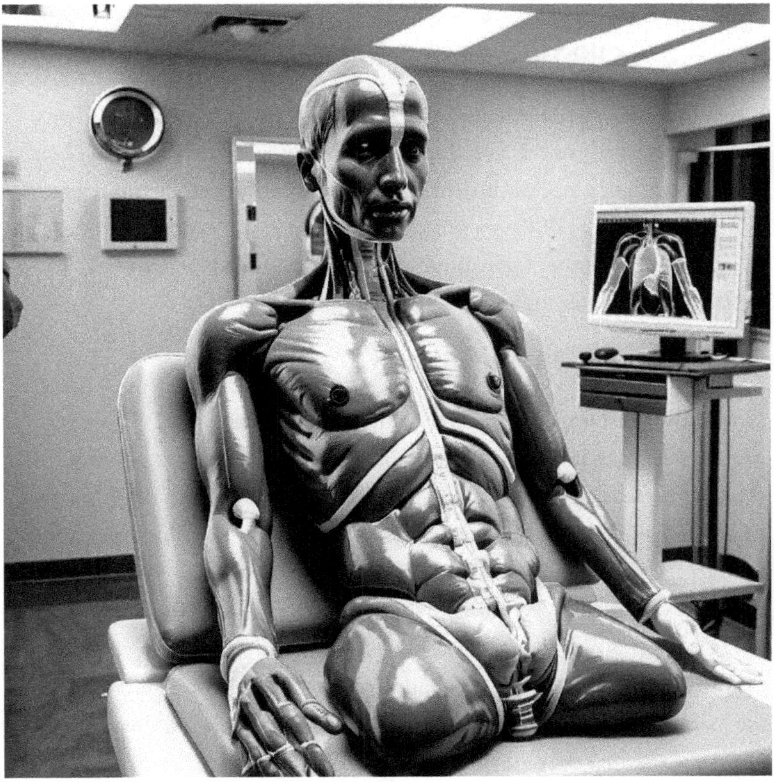

Fig. 6. Trauma victim and basic life support

BLS for trauma victims requires adaptations to standard CPR protocols to prevent further injury and to address the specific needs of the victim. Trauma patients present complex challenges, and high-quality chest compressions, airway management, and bleeding control are essential components of care. By understanding and applying these modifications, responders can improve the likelihood of survival and minimize the potential for additional harm. It is vital for responders to remain calm, assess the situation thoroughly, and make necessary adjustments to standard BLS techniques based on the nature of the trauma and the victim's condition.

SECTION II

CPR Techniques for Pregnant Patients

Cardiopulmonary resuscitation (CPR) techniques for pregnant patients require special considerations due to the physiological changes that occur during pregnancy and the potential risks to both the mother and the fetus. When performing CPR on a pregnant individual, it is essential to adapt the standard CPR protocols to optimize the chances of survival for both the mother and the unborn child.

1. Positioning the Pregnant Patient

One of the most important adjustments when performing CPR on a pregnant woman is the positioning. As the pregnancy progresses, the growing uterus can compress the major blood vessels, especially when the patient is lying flat on their back. This compression can reduce blood flow to both the mother and the fetus, making it more challenging to maintain adequate circulation. To mitigate this, the patient should be tilted to the left side. This position, known as the "left lateral tilt," helps alleviate pressure on the inferior vena cava, the large vein that returns blood from the lower body to the heart. This tilt allows for better blood flow and improves the chances of both maternal and fetal survival.

- If the patient is in the later stages of pregnancy, typically after 20 weeks, a wedge or other support should be placed under the right hip or the right side of the body to ensure the patient is adequately tilted. This adjustment helps to maintain optimal circulation and prevent hypotension.

2. Performing Chest Compressions

The technique for chest compressions during CPR on a pregnant woman is generally the same as for a non-pregnant adult, but it is important to ensure that compressions are applied with enough force to effectively circulate blood. The depth and rate of compressions should be in accordance with current CPR guidelines—at least 2 inches deep at a rate of 100 to 120 compressions per minute.

However, rescuers should be aware of the increased size of the abdomen and adjust their position to avoid any unnecessary pressure on the uterus or fetus. It's crucial to focus on proper hand placement, ensuring that compressions are performed on the lower half of the sternum, as in regular CPR.

3. Rescue Breathing

When performing rescue breathing on a pregnant patient, the technique remains the same as standard CPR. Ensure that the airway is open by tilting the head back and lifting the chin, and provide two rescue breaths. If there is no response after chest compressions and rescue breaths, continue CPR with a focus on high-quality chest compressions and minimal interruption. The key is to maintain adequate ventilation and circulation, which will help sustain oxygen levels for both the mother and the fetus.

4. Defibrillation

In cases where an automated external defibrillator (AED) is available, it should be used as quickly as possible, just as with any adult patient. There are no modifications needed for the use of an AED on a pregnant woman. The shock is delivered to the chest as per the usual protocol, aiming to restore a normal heart rhythm. It's important to ensure that the AED pads are properly placed on the chest, ensuring that the shock is directed through the heart.

- It is safe to use an AED on a pregnant patient, and the shock will not harm the fetus. In fact, restoring normal cardiac rhythm is crucial for both maternal and fetal survival.

5. Special Considerations in Advanced Pregnancy

In later stages of pregnancy, especially after 24 weeks, additional considerations may be necessary. In case of a pregnant woman's cardiac arrest, it is critical to rapidly proceed with CPR, but once the fetus is viable, the importance of rapid delivery may also come into play. If the mother's pulse cannot be restored and advanced medical help arrives, they may initiate emergency measures to deliver the baby, which can be critical in cases of maternal death. In these situations, the priority is still to provide effective CPR to the mother while preparing for the possibility of cesarean delivery in a hospital setting.

6. Maternal and Fetal Resuscitation

CPR for pregnant patients also includes consideration of fetal well-being. During resuscitation, efforts should be made to maintain circulation to the uterus. If resuscitation is not successful, emergency cesarean delivery should be considered, especially if the fetus is viable. After 20 weeks of pregnancy, the fetus may still benefit from the mother's CPR, even if the mother's chances of survival are minimal, by preserving oxygenated blood flow to the uterus.

7. Role of the Rescuers

When performing CPR on a pregnant patient, the rescuers should ensure that they are able to perform high-quality CPR continuously. If two rescuers are present, one should continue chest compressions while the other administers rescue breaths and prepares for defibrillation or advanced medical support. The physical demands of CPR may be more taxing, so it is crucial to swap out rescuers every 2 minutes to prevent fatigue, which could compromise the effectiveness of the compressions.

In essence, performing CPR on a pregnant patient requires some adaptation of standard CPR techniques. The primary difference is the positioning of the patient to relieve pressure on the major blood vessels, which ensures better circulation for both the mother and the fetus. Other considerations include the application of high-quality chest compressions, the use of an AED, and appropriate rescue breathing. As with any CPR situation, the goal is to maintain circulation and oxygenation as effectively as possible until advanced medical care arrives. Understanding and applying these modifications can significantly improve the chances of survival for both the pregnant patient and the unborn child.

SECTION III

Managing Overcrowded Environments and Limited Resources

Managing overcrowded environments and limited resources during a medical emergency requires strategic prioritization, adaptability, and effective communication. In situations where there are many patients or limited medical supplies—such as natural disasters, large public gatherings, or high-traffic healthcare facilities—emergency responders and healthcare providers must be prepared to deliver efficient care under challenging circumstances. To optimize patient outcomes, responders need to implement rapid assessment techniques, resource allocation strategies, and, where possible, rely on community support.

One of the first steps in managing an overcrowded environment is triage, a process of prioritizing patients based on the severity of their condition. Triage enables healthcare providers to quickly identify patients with life-threatening injuries or conditions, allowing for the most urgent cases to receive immediate attention. For example, in the context of Basic Life Support (BLS), patients in cardiac or respiratory arrest are prioritized for interventions like CPR and defibrillation. This rapid assessment ensures that critical resources, such as oxygen and Automated External Defibrillators (AEDs), are directed to those who need them most urgently, while other patients with stable conditions can be attended to as resources allow.

Communication and coordination among responders are also critical in such environments. Clear, direct communication helps to organize and delegate tasks, reducing confusion and duplication of effort. Assigning roles, such as airway management, chest compressions, and crowd control, allows responders to maintain order and optimize the use of available personnel. Effective team dynamics are essential; team members should communicate patient updates, equipment needs, and changing conditions promptly, ensuring smooth transitions and continuous care without interruptions.

In environments with limited medical resources, creative solutions and improvisation may be necessary to ensure that as many patients as possible receive effective care. For instance, if there is a shortage of resuscitation equipment or AEDs, rotating and sharing devices across teams may be required. Improvised tools, such as using manual chest compressions in lieu of mechanical devices or creating makeshift airway aids, can help sustain patients when standard equipment is unavailable. BLS providers are trained to adapt quickly, using available tools to create functional solutions that maintain patient care standards while minimizing risks.

Furthermore, in scenarios with limited resources, it's beneficial to involve bystanders or minimally trained individuals who can assist with non-technical tasks, such as guiding crowds, providing basic information to responders, or comforting stable patients. Bystanders can also assist with tasks like chest compressions if they are confident and willing to help, allowing healthcare providers to focus on more technical aspects of patient care. Community preparedness and awareness are therefore invaluable, as even basic CPR knowledge in the public can provide additional support and buy time for responders.

Managing an overcrowded environment also requires constant assessment and flexibility. Responders must continuously monitor the availability of supplies and personnel to determine when adjustments to care plans are needed. This might involve deciding to shift focus from one patient to another based on changes in their conditions or on the availability of resources. By maintaining a high level of situational awareness, providers can make real-time decisions that maximize resource utilization and patient outcomes.

Documentation and reporting are other essential aspects, even in crowded settings. Keeping track of patients, interventions, and available supplies can prevent duplication of care or loss of crucial data needed for ongoing management and later review. Recording patient information, such as response times and treatments provided, can help responders track outcomes, streamline care transitions, and provide insight for future planning in similar situations.

Finally, post-event debriefing is valuable for teams working in overcrowded, resource-limited environments. Reflecting on what went well, identifying areas for improvement, and discussing emotional impacts can help responders prepare for future scenarios, enhance morale, and foster resilience among the team. Proper planning and continuous training in managing high-stress, resource-constrained environments help BLS providers and other healthcare workers maintain readiness and ensure they can deliver life-saving care, even in challenging situations.

Managing overcrowded environments and limited resources requires skill, flexibility, and collaboration. With careful triage, communication, improvisation, and the support of bystanders, BLS providers can help optimize patient care, reduce the strain on resources, and maximize survival outcomes in critical situations.

SECTION IV

Considerations for Drowning and Drug Overdose Cases

When performing Basic Life Support (BLS) in cases of drowning or drug overdose, certain considerations must be taken into account to adapt standard protocols and improve the chances of survival. These situations involve unique physiological challenges, such as hypoxia in drowning or respiratory depression in overdose, which may require modifications to traditional BLS techniques.

Here are the key considerations for each scenario:

1. Drowning

- Primary Cause of Cardiac Arrest: In drowning cases, cardiac arrest typically results from severe hypoxia (oxygen deprivation) caused by water obstructing the airway. As such, oxygenation is a priority.
- Initial Assessment and Rescue Breaths: Unlike traditional BLS, which often emphasizes starting with chest compressions, it is essential to begin with rescue breaths for drowning victims. Delivering two initial rescue breaths helps oxygenate the blood, which is especially critical in drowning.
- Effective Ventilations: Since oxygenation is compromised, ensure that the rescue breaths are delivered effectively with each breath lasting about 1 second. Watch for the chest to rise to confirm that air is reaching the lungs.
- Positioning and Spine Precautions: Drowning can occur due to diving injuries or water-related accidents that may involve spinal injuries. Take care when moving the victim, especially if spinal trauma is suspected, and consider using a jaw-thrust maneuver to open the airway without moving the neck.
- Continuous Compressions with Ventilations: After the initial rescue breaths, follow a standard cycle of 30 compressions to 2 breaths if performing one-rescuer CPR. If trained, consider using continuous compressions with ventilations to maintain oxygenation.
- AED Use: AEDs should be used as soon as they become available. In drowning cases, cardiac arrest rhythms may respond well to defibrillation, so timely AED application can be beneficial.
- Post-Resuscitation Care: After a successful resuscitation, continue to monitor the victim's respiratory status and prepare for potential complications, such as secondary drowning, where water in the lungs can impair breathing even after initial recovery.

2. Drug Overdose

- Primary Cause of Cardiac Arrest: Cardiac arrest in overdose cases is frequently caused by respiratory depression, especially with opioid overdoses. This can lead to hypoxia, which in turn causes the heart to stop.
- Assess for Responsiveness and Breathing: For an overdose victim who is unresponsive and not breathing or only gasping, begin CPR immediately. If breathing is present but shallow or irregular, rescue breathing can be initiated without compressions until help arrives.
- Administration of Naloxone (if available): If an opioid overdose is suspected and naloxone (Narcan) is available, administer it as soon as possible. Naloxone can temporarily reverse the effects of opioids, restoring normal breathing. Administer it intranasally or intramuscularly according to local protocols, but do not delay CPR while waiting for its effects.
- Ventilation and Oxygen Support: Respiratory support is crucial in drug overdose cases. Ensure that rescue breaths are delivered effectively, and consider using a barrier device or bag-valve-mask if available and you are trained to do so.
- Chest Compressions: If the patient has no pulse, follow standard CPR guidelines with chest compressions at a rate of 100 to 120 per minute, alternating with rescue breaths at a 30:2 ratio. For two-rescuer CPR, coordinate to provide high-quality ventilations along with compressions.
- AED Use: Apply an AED as soon as it's available, especially if the person has become pulseless. Drug overdoses may induce cardiac arrhythmias that can be shockable, so AED analysis is essential.
- Monitor for Recurrent Respiratory Depression: Opioid overdoses, in particular, may require repeated doses of naloxone due to the duration of opioid effects. Continue to monitor respiratory and cardiac status, as recurrent respiratory depression can occur after naloxone's effects wear off.

Both drowning and drug overdose cases require prompt intervention and adaptations to traditional BLS techniques. By understanding these considerations, rescuers can tailor their approach to maximize survival outcomes in these specific emergencies.

EXERCISE VI

1. When performing CPR on a pregnant patient, where should you place your hands for chest compressions?

   a. Slightly higher on the sternum than usual

   b. At the same location as for non-pregnant adults

   c. Directly over the abdomen

   d. On the lower part of the ribcage

2. In cases of drowning, what is the first priority when performing BLS?

   a. Drying the patient before starting CPR

   b. Providing rescue breaths immediately

   c. Checking for external injuries

   d. Administering an AED

3. How should chest compressions be modified for a trauma victim with a suspected spinal injury?

   a. Avoid compressions entirely

   b. Use one hand for compressions

   c. Maintain spinal alignment while performing compressions

   d. Perform compressions at a slower rate

4. For a patient with a tracheostomy tube, how should rescue breaths be delivered?

a. Through the nose

b. Using a bag-mask device over the tracheostomy

c. By sealing the mouth and nose

d. Through a nasal cannula

5. What is the recommended depth of chest compressions for an infant?

a. At least 2 inches (5 cm)

b. Approximately 1.5 inches (4 cm)

c. At least 3 inches (7.5 cm)

d. Approximately 1 inch (2.5 cm)

6. In a choking pregnant patient who becomes unresponsive, what is the immediate next step?

a. Perform abdominal thrusts

b. Begin chest compressions

c. Check for and remove visible obstructions

d. Administer back blows

7. Which adjustment should be made when using an AED on a child under 8 years old?

a. Use standard adult pads in all cases

b. Use pediatric pads if available

c. Place the pads over the stomach

d. Avoid using an AED entirely

8. When performing CPR on a patient with a pacemaker, how should AED pads be placed?

a. Directly over the pacemaker

b. Avoid placing pads on the chest

c. At least 1 inch away from the pacemaker device

d. Over the ribcage, avoiding the sternum

9. What is the most appropriate action for a choking infant who is conscious but cannot cry or cough?

a. Perform abdominal thrusts

b. Deliver 5 back blows followed by 5 chest thrusts

c. Administer CPR immediately

d. Wait for the infant to cough up the obstruction

10. In a patient experiencing cardiac arrest due to hypothermia, which modification should be considered?

a. Avoid using an AED

b. Perform rapid chest compressions only

c. Perform CPR and wait until the patient is warm before defibrillation

d. Focus on warming the patient and delay CPR

11. For a drowning victim, how should ventilation be initiated during CPR?

a. Start with chest compressions

b. Deliver 5 initial rescue breaths before chest compressions

c. Alternate between back blows and compressions

d. Only provide chest compressions

12. In trauma patients with severe bleeding, what should be prioritized during BLS?

a. Controlling bleeding before chest compressions

b. Performing chest compressions immediately

c. Checking for fractures before starting CPR

d. Avoiding any intervention until EMS arrives

13. For an opioid overdose patient in cardiac arrest, what additional measure is recommended?

a. Providing naloxone while continuing CPR

b. Using an AED immediately

c. Only performing rescue breaths

d. Waiting for advanced medical care before intervention

14. How should chest compressions be performed for a bariatric patient?

a. On the upper abdomen

b. At the center of the sternum, with deeper compressions if needed

c. With reduced force due to patient size

d. On the side of the chest

15. When performing CPR in a confined space, what is the best approach?

a. Wait for the patient to be moved to an open area

b. Perform CPR in the available space while ensuring safety

c. Avoid chest compressions until more help arrives

d. Focus only on rescue breaths

16. In cases of suspected electrocution, what should be checked before beginning CPR?

a. The patient's pulse

b. The safety of the scene and deactivation of the power source

c. The patient's temperature

d. Availability of an AED

17. What is a key consideration when performing CPR on a patient with severe chest trauma?

a. Perform compressions at a slower rate

b. Avoid compressions and focus on rescue breaths

c. Use the same compression technique but expect potential complications

d. Compress over the ribs rather than the sternum

18. When treating an unconscious choking child, what step follows 30 chest compressions?

a. Perform a blind finger sweep

b. Check the mouth for a visible obstruction

c. Deliver 5 rescue breaths

d. Administer an AED

19. For a pregnant patient, why is left lateral uterine displacement recommended?

a. To facilitate blood flow and reduce pressure on the aorta and vena cava

b. To stabilize the spine during compressions

c. To make chest compressions easier to perform

d. To prevent uterine rupture during CPR

20. How should CPR be adapted for a patient with severe hypothermia?

a. Avoid performing rescue breaths

b. Use minimal chest compressions to avoid damaging the chest

c. Continue CPR but avoid rapid defibrillation until the patient is rewarmed

d. Focus solely on warming the patient

CHAPTER EIGHT

Team Dynamics and High-Performance BLS

SECTION I

Role of Team-Based BLS

The role of team-based Basic Life Support (BLS) is to provide a coordinated and effective response to life-threatening emergencies. When multiple rescuers are available, working as a team allows for better management of critical tasks, minimizes responder fatigue, and improves overall patient outcomes. Effective teamwork in BLS requires communication, role delegation, and cooperation.

The key components involved in team-based BLS:

1. Clear Role Assignment

In team-based BLS, each team member is assigned specific roles based on their skills and experience. Roles might include chest compressor, airway manager, AED operator, and team leader. Assigning these roles from the outset prevents confusion and ensures that each task is managed efficiently. For example, one rescuer may perform chest compressions while another handles ventilation, and a third manages the AED. This division of labor allows each member to focus on their specific tasks, leading to higher-quality care.

2. Effective Communication

Clear and concise communication is essential in team-based BLS. The team leader or any member giving instructions must use simple, direct language and confirm that each team member understands their responsibilities. Closed-loop communication, where instructions are repeated back for confirmation, ensures that commands are heard and understood correctly. For example, if the team leader says, "Start compressions," the chest compressor should respond with "Starting compressions" to confirm. Good communication minimizes errors and helps maintain a calm, organized environment.

3. Strong Leadership

A designated team leader plays a crucial role in coordinating the team's actions. The team leader assesses the situation, monitors the patient's condition, and oversees the quality of interventions such as chest compressions, ventilation, and AED use. They also ensure that team members adhere to the latest BLS guidelines, prioritize tasks, and address any issues that arise. In many cases, the team leader may also be responsible for updating EMS personnel upon their arrival, summarizing the actions taken, and any notable changes in the patient's condition.

4. High-Performance CPR through Role Switching

Team-based BLS allows for rotating roles to maintain the quality of compressions and prevent rescuer fatigue. Chest compressions are physically demanding, and without role rotation, a single rescuer's performance may decline over time. Ideally, rescuers should switch roles every 2 minutes or after five cycles of CPR, allowing each team member to remain effective. When rotating roles, team members should communicate clearly and ensure a smooth transition to avoid any interruption in compressions.

5. Minimizing Interruptions in Chest Compressions

One of the main advantages of team-based BLS is the ability to minimize interruptions in chest compressions, which is critical for maintaining blood flow to the brain and heart. By having dedicated roles and smooth role-switching protocols, team members can work together to keep pauses to a minimum. For example, while one rescuer is providing chest compressions, another rescuer can prepare the AED, ensuring that defibrillation can occur quickly and efficiently with minimal downtime in compressions.

6. Coordination with AED and Advanced Airway Management

In a team-based approach, specific members can focus on managing the AED and monitoring the patient's airway. The AED operator prepares the device, places the pads, and delivers shocks as indicated, allowing the chest compressor to maintain continuous CPR until the AED advises a shock. Similarly, a rescuer designated as the airway manager ensures open airways and proper ventilation, which is especially important for patients who are not breathing. This role may involve providing breaths with a bag-valve-mask (BVM) or administering an advanced airway device if trained and available.

7. Monitoring Quality of Care

In team-based BLS, team members can provide feedback to each other to maintain the quality of care. For example, if chest compressions are not deep enough, a team member can offer a reminder or adjust technique. The team leader, in particular, monitors the quality of chest compressions, the rate of ventilations, and adherence to timing for AED shocks. Ongoing feedback helps ensure that each BLS intervention is performed at the highest possible standard.

8. Preparation for Handover to EMS

The team-based approach also facilitates a smooth handover when EMS arrives. The team leader should be prepared to provide a clear and concise summary, including the initial patient assessment, the interventions performed, the time of AED shocks, and any changes in the patient's condition. Having a team member assigned to track the timing and sequence of interventions can make this process smoother. An organized handover allows EMS to quickly understand the patient's status and continue life-saving efforts seamlessly.

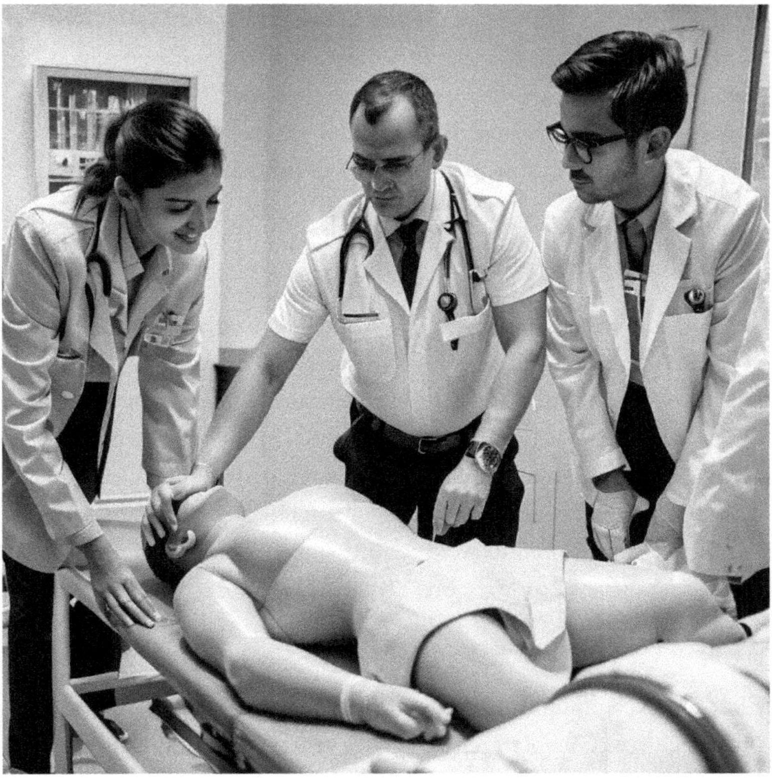

Fig. 7. Role of Team-Based in basic life support

In summary, team-based BLS improves the quality of emergency care by dividing tasks, reducing responder fatigue, and ensuring continuous, high-quality CPR. Through effective role assignment, strong leadership, and good communication, a well-coordinated team can deliver superior patient care, significantly enhancing the likelihood of survival in critical emergencies.

SECTION II

Effective Communication in Resuscitation

Effective communication is vital in resuscitation situations, where quick, clear, and accurate information exchange can significantly impact the success of the intervention and the patient's outcome. During resuscitation, team members often need to perform different tasks simultaneously, making communication the cornerstone of coordination. Effective communication helps ensure that each team member understands their role, anticipates the next steps, and provides feedback as the situation evolves.

1. Establishing Clear Roles and Leadership

At the start of a resuscitation effort, it is essential to establish clear roles and designate a team leader. The leader is responsible for overseeing the entire process, delegating tasks, and ensuring that team members remain focused and coordinated. When everyone knows who is in charge, communication becomes more structured, and the team can respond more efficiently. The team leader should communicate assignments clearly, using names or specific role designations to avoid confusion. For example, "Alex, continue chest compressions," or "Sara, prepare the AED."

2. Closed-Loop Communication

Closed-loop communication is a critical technique in resuscitation and emergency care. It involves repeating back orders to confirm that they were heard and understood correctly. When a team leader gives an instruction, the team member receiving the instruction should repeat it back, and the leader should acknowledge the confirmation. For instance, the leader might say, "Administer 1 mg of epinephrine," and the responder would confirm, "Administering 1 mg of epinephrine." This technique ensures that instructions are clear and reduces the risk of misunderstandings, especially in a high-stress environment.

3. Clear, Concise, and Direct Language

In resuscitation scenarios, there is no room for ambiguous or vague language. Communication should be clear, concise, and direct. Avoiding unnecessary words and using specific terms helps prevent confusion and misunderstandings. For example, instead of saying "Could you get that over here?" a team member might say, "Bring the AED here now." Simple, specific language helps everyone on the team understand exactly what is needed without room for interpretation.

4. Use of Standardized Terminology

Consistent use of standardized terminology is essential, as it minimizes confusion and ensures that all team members interpret instructions in the same way. Terms like "start compressions," "defibrillate," "administer epinephrine," or "check pulse" have precise meanings in a medical context. Avoiding slang or unfamiliar jargon prevents misunderstandings and keeps everyone on the same page. This is particularly important in resuscitation, where each second counts, and errors can be costly.

5. Frequent Updates and Progress Reports

Regular status updates and progress reports keep the team informed about the patient's condition and the ongoing actions. During resuscitation, it is crucial for team members to continually report changes in the patient's condition, such as return of spontaneous circulation (ROSC) or deterioration in vital signs. The team leader might ask, "What's the pulse status?" or "Are compressions effective?" Team members should be prepared to provide quick, accurate updates, allowing the leader to make informed decisions based on the latest information.

6. Supportive and Respectful Interactions

Resuscitation can be a high-stress situation, so maintaining respectful and supportive communication is essential. Team members should avoid harsh or judgmental language, even when things become challenging. A calm and composed tone can help alleviate tension, reduce errors caused by stress, and promote an environment where each team member feels supported and motivated to do their best. For example, if a team member misses a step, constructive feedback like, "Let's try a bit more chest recoil next time," helps correct the action without discouraging the provider.

7. Encouraging Open Feedback and Clarification

During resuscitation, team members should feel comfortable asking questions and providing feedback if they are unsure of an instruction or notice something unusual. Encouraging open communication allows individuals to clarify misunderstandings immediately, reducing the risk of errors. For example, if a team member is unsure about the correct dose of a medication, they should feel empowered to ask, "Did you confirm 1 mg of epinephrine?" Open dialogue helps maintain a safe, efficient, and collaborative resuscitation environment.

8. Debriefing After the Event

After a resuscitation event, a structured debriefing session can provide the team an opportunity to reflect on the experience, discuss what went well, and identify areas for improvement. This debriefing can involve a review of communication practices, coordination, and specific technical skills used during the resuscitation. A debrief allows team members to learn from the experience, enhancing their skills and preparedness for future emergencies. The team leader might guide the debrief by asking, "What could we improve next time?" or "How did our communication help or hinder the process?"

In summary, effective communication in resuscitation is built on clear leadership, closed-loop communication, concise language, standardized terminology, and supportive interactions. By following these principles, resuscitation teams can work more efficiently and effectively, reducing the risk of errors and improving the patient's chance of a positive outcome. These communication skills are not only valuable in emergencies but are essential for building trust, teamwork, and a culture of excellence in emergency response.

SECTION III

Coordinating Roles in Multi-Provider Resuscitation

Coordinating roles in multi-provider resuscitation is vital to ensure the highest quality of care during a cardiac arrest or similar emergency situation. When multiple rescuers are available, efficient teamwork and clear role delegation can reduce interruptions, maintain high-quality CPR, and increase the patient's chances of survival. Each team member should understand their role, communicate effectively, and coordinate actions to maximize efficiency. Here's a breakdown of how to organize and coordinate roles in a multi-provider resuscitation effort:

1. Assigning Team Roles

In multi-provider resuscitation, specific roles are typically assigned to streamline tasks and avoid confusion. Common roles include:

- Team Leader: Oversees the entire resuscitation process, making sure tasks are coordinated, assessing the situation, and giving instructions to other team members. The team leader should also monitor the quality of CPR and adjust team actions as needed.
- Compressor: Provides continuous chest compressions, focusing on proper depth and rate, and ensuring full chest recoil between compressions. The compressor should be rotated every 2 minutes to avoid fatigue.
- Ventilator: Manages rescue breaths, either by using a bag-valve-mask (BVM) or by delivering mouth-to-mask breaths, if applicable. This person works closely with the compressor to ensure breaths are delivered at the appropriate times, minimizing interruptions.
- AED Operator: Prepares and operates the Automated External Defibrillator (AED), applying pads, analyzing rhythm, and delivering shocks when prompted. This person is also responsible for announcing "clear" to ensure team safety before delivering shocks.

2. Establishing Effective Communication

Effective communication is key in multi-provider resuscitation. The team leader should communicate clearly and concisely, using direct commands such as "Start compressions," "Prepare the AED," or "Switch positions in 5 seconds." Team members should respond verbally with "Yes" or "Got it" to confirm they understand. Closed-loop communication, where each team member acknowledges their task verbally, helps prevent misunderstandings and ensures all tasks are completed accurately.

3. Maintaining Continuous CPR with Regular Switches

To maintain high-quality chest compressions, the compressor should switch roles every 2 minutes or sooner if fatigue sets in. The team leader should monitor the time and announce the switch just before the 2-minute mark, allowing the backup compressor to be ready. When switching, the backup compressor should take over without any delay in compressions, maintaining the correct rhythm and minimizing interruptions.

4. AED Use and Safety Protocol

The AED operator plays a critical role in safely administering defibrillation when needed. Once the AED is set up, the operator should follow AED prompts, announcing "clear" to alert the team to stay away from the patient before delivering a shock. The team leader should ensure everyone follows this command to avoid accidental shock. After defibrillation, compressions should resume immediately to avoid any delay in CPR.

5. Managing the Airway and Delivering Effective Breaths

The ventilator is responsible for maintaining the patient's airway and delivering breaths at appropriate intervals. Ideally, the ventilator should use a bag-valve mask, especially if trained in its use, to provide effective ventilation. The ventilator should coordinate with the compressor to ensure breaths are given every 30 compressions in a single-rescuer scenario or every 15 compressions if two rescuers are handling CPR for a pediatric patient.

6. Monitoring CPR Quality and Providing Feedback

The team leader should observe the quality of CPR and provide immediate feedback if improvements are needed. For example, if compressions are too shallow or not fast enough, the team leader should instruct the compressor to adjust. Likewise, if breaths are not effective or there is too much delay in switching roles, the team leader should address these issues to optimize resuscitation efforts.

7. Anticipating and Preparing for Changes in Patient Status

Throughout resuscitation, the team should be alert for any changes in the patient's status, such as signs of return of spontaneous circulation (ROSC). The team leader should be prepared to direct other team members to reassess the patient, check for a pulse, and adjust treatment accordingly if the patient begins to respond. Having each team member aware of potential changes helps the team respond quickly and effectively.

8. Debriefing After Resuscitation

After the resuscitation event, a debriefing session is essential for evaluating performance, identifying areas for improvement, and providing emotional support to the team. Each member should have an opportunity to discuss their role and share insights. The debriefing should focus on what went well, what challenges arose, and any improvements needed for future resuscitations.

In multi-provider resuscitation, effective coordination and clear role assignments reduce confusion, improve CPR quality, and optimize patient outcomes. Each team member's ability to perform their role while maintaining open communication and mutual support is crucial to a successful resuscitation effort.

SECTION IV

Steps to Achieve High-Performance BLS

High-performance Basic Life Support (BLS) refers to the coordinated and optimized execution of resuscitation techniques to maximize a patient's chances of survival during life-threatening emergencies. Achieving high-performance BLS requires adherence to best practices, effective teamwork, and precise execution of skills. The following steps outline how to achieve high-performance BLS:

1. Ensure Scene Safety

- Before initiating care, assess the scene for potential hazards to ensure the safety of both the patient and rescuers.
- Quickly determine whether the environment is safe for performing BLS or if the patient needs to be moved to a safer location.

2. Recognize the Emergency and Call for Help

- Assess the patient for unresponsiveness by tapping their shoulder and shouting.
- Check for normal breathing and a pulse for no more than 10 seconds.
- If the patient is unresponsive and not breathing normally (or only gasping), immediately activate emergency medical services (EMS) or have someone else do so.
- Retrieve or request an automated external defibrillator (AED) while preparing to begin CPR.

3. Perform High-Quality Chest Compressions

- Position yourself at the patient's side, place the heel of one hand on the center of the chest (lower half of the sternum), and the other hand on top.
- Compress the chest to a depth of at least 2 inches (5 cm) for adults, allowing full chest recoil between compressions.
- Perform compressions at a rate of 100 to 120 per minute, ensuring consistent depth and rhythm.
- Avoid leaning on the chest during recoil to maintain effective blood circulation.

4. Deliver Effective Rescue Breaths

- After 30 chest compressions, open the airway using the head-tilt, chin-lift technique.

- Deliver 2 breaths using a pocket mask or bag-mask device, ensuring each breath lasts about 1 second and causes visible chest rise.
- Avoid excessive ventilation, which can lead to complications such as decreased cardiac output or gastric inflation.

5. Minimize Interruptions in Compressions

- Strive to keep interruptions in chest compressions to less than 10 seconds.
- Coordinate rescue breathing and AED use to minimize downtime between compressions.
- Prepare all necessary equipment (such as AED pads) in advance to reduce delays.

6. Utilize an Automated External Defibrillator (AED)

- Turn on the AED as soon as it is available and follow the device's prompts.
- Apply the AED pads to the patient's bare chest according to the diagrams on the pads.
- If a shockable rhythm is detected, ensure no one is touching the patient and deliver the shock.
- Immediately resume chest compressions after the shock or if the AED advises no shock.

7. Incorporate Team-Based CPR for Efficiency

- If multiple rescuers are available, assign roles to ensure seamless care (e.g., one person performs compressions, another handles ventilation, and a third manages the AED).
- Rotate rescuers performing chest compressions every 2 minutes to prevent fatigue and maintain high-quality compressions.
- Use clear and direct communication to coordinate efforts and avoid confusion.

8. Adapt to Special Circumstances

- For trauma patients, drowning victims, or pregnant individuals, adjust techniques as needed while adhering to BLS principles.
- Be aware of unique challenges, such as managing obstructed airways or performing compressions on a smaller frame (e.g., children or infants).

9. Continuously Monitor and Reassess

- Regularly reassess the patient's condition to determine if there are any signs of return of spontaneous circulation (ROSC), such as breathing or a detectable pulse.
- Be prepared to transition to post-resuscitation care if the patient regains circulation.

10. Stay Calm and Focused

- In high-stress situations, maintaining composure allows for precise and efficient execution of BLS steps.
- Practice regular BLS training and scenarios to build confidence and competence.

By following these steps, BLS providers can deliver high-performance resuscitation, optimizing the chances of survival and recovery for patients experiencing cardiac arrest or other critical emergencies. Regular practice, adherence to guidelines, and effective teamwork are essential for maintaining proficiency and ensuring the best possible outcomes.

EXERCISE VII

1. What is the primary benefit of effective team dynamics during a resuscitation attempt?

A. Faster transport to the hospital

B. Minimization of confusion and errors

C. Reduction in the need for CPR

D. Avoiding the use of an AED

2. Which of the following is a characteristic of high-performing resuscitation teams?

A. Independent decision-making by each team member

B. A clear leader and defined roles

C. Constant reassigning of roles during CPR

D. Avoiding communication to reduce distractions

3. During a multi-provider resuscitation, what is the role of the team leader?

A. Perform chest compressions throughout the resuscitation

B. Direct and coordinate the actions of the team

C. Operate the AED exclusively

D. Provide rescue breaths only

4. How often should rescuers performing chest compressions switch roles to avoid fatigue?

A. Every 30 seconds

B. Every 1 minute

C. Every 2 minutes

D. Every 5 minutes

5. What is the primary goal of high-performance BLS?

A. To ensure each team member has equal responsibilities

B. To maximize survival rates and minimize errors

C. To avoid the use of advanced medical equipment

D. To simplify resuscitation by reducing team size

6. What is the recommended way to communicate in a high-performing team?

A. Whisper to avoid overwhelming other team members

B. Use clear, concise, and direct communication

C. Assign nonverbal cues for instructions

D. Only communicate when directly asked by the leader

7. When coordinating multi-provider CPR, what should the AED operator focus on?

A. Delivering shocks immediately after compressions

B. Minimizing interruptions in chest compressions

C. Performing rescue breaths simultaneously with defibrillation

D. Providing feedback on chest compression depth

8. What is the benefit of assigning specific roles in a resuscitation team?

A. Reducing the need for team training

B. Allowing individual members to work independently

C. Enhancing efficiency and minimizing delays

D. Limiting the use of AEDs

9. Which of the following actions demonstrates closed-loop communication?

A. Team members acting without confirmation of orders

B. Repeating back instructions to confirm understanding

C. Assigning roles without team input

D. Avoiding verbal responses to commands

10. How does frequent training improve team dynamics in BLS?

A. It reduces the need for AEDs in emergencies

B. It eliminates the need for a team leader

C. It enhances teamwork and role familiarity

D. It removes the need for individual decision-making

11. What is the primary task of the team member performing chest compressions?

A. Ensuring complete chest recoil and proper depth

B. Monitoring the AED for shock readiness

C. Coordinating team communication

D. Giving rescue breaths every 30 seconds

12. What is the most important step for the team leader when an additional team member arrives?

A. Reassess the patient's pulse

B. Assign them a specific role to fill

C. Wait until the next cycle of compressions to integrate them

D. Have them replace the AED operator

13. What is a critical component of high-performance CPR?

A. Maintaining a compression rate below 100 per minute

B. Pausing compressions for every rescue breath

C. Minimizing interruptions in compressions

D. Rotating roles every 5 minutes

14. What should a rescuer do if they are unable to perform chest compressions effectively due to fatigue?

A. Continue compressions until directed to stop

B. Ask another team member to switch roles

C. Wait for the AED to deliver a shock before stopping

D. Pause and reassess the patient

15. How can a team member provide effective feedback during a resuscitation?

A. By pointing out mistakes in a harsh tone

B. By providing constructive, specific, and timely suggestions

C. By remaining silent to avoid disrupting the team

D. By waiting until after the resuscitation to provide input

16. Which of the following is a sign of poor team dynamics?

A. Clear assignment of roles

B. Frequent interruptions during CPR

C. Use of closed-loop communication

D. Switching roles every 2 minutes

17. What is the ideal way to handle disagreements within the team during resuscitation?

A. Pause the resuscitation to discuss the issue

B. Follow the team leader's decision and resolve disagreements later

C. Allow team members to act independently without coordination

D. Ignore the disagreement and continue resuscitation silently

18. Why is rapid role rotation important in high-performance BLS?

A. To allow each team member to practice every skill

B. To ensure that rescuers do not become fatigued

C. To maintain a steady pace of compressions without communication

D. To reduce the reliance on AEDs

19. What is the significance of providing debriefing after a resuscitation event?

A. It helps team members improve skills and address challenges

B. It eliminates the need for future team training

C. It replaces the need for regular CPR certification

D. It ensures the AED is always ready for use

20. Which aspect of team dynamics ensures all team members understand their tasks?

A. Independent decision-making

B. Strong leadership and role assignment

C. Minimizing verbal communication during resuscitation

D. Allowing team members to self-assign roles

ANSWERS TO EXERCISES

EXERCISE I – ANSWERS

1. The primary goal of BLS is to preserve life by maintaining circulation and breathing in individuals experiencing cardiac arrest or other life-threatening emergencies until advanced care is available.

2. The rescuer should assess the scene for safety to ensure it is safe to approach and provide care without endangering themselves or others.

3. Ensuring scene safety prevents the rescuer from becoming a victim and allows them to provide uninterrupted care to the patient.

4. Tap the individual on the shoulder and shout, "Are you okay?" while observing for any movement or reaction.

5. No more than 10 seconds.

6. Activate emergency medical services (EMS) by calling 911 (or the local emergency number) and begin CPR immediately.

7. Minimizing interruptions ensures continuous blood flow to vital organs, increasing the chance of survival.

8. Early recognition and activation of EMS, early CPR, early defibrillation, effective advanced care, and post-resuscitation care.

9. High-quality CPR focuses on optimal depth, rate, minimal interruptions, and full chest recoil to maximize blood circulation and oxygen delivery.

10. Gloves, masks, and eye protection are recommended to reduce the risk of exposure to infectious materials.

11. The compression-to-ventilation ratio is 30:2.

12. At least 2 inches (5 cm).

13. 100 to 120 compressions per minute.

14. Full chest recoil allows the heart to refill with blood, maximizing the effectiveness of each compression.

15. To open the airway by lifting the tongue away from the back of the throat.

16. An AED should be used as soon as it becomes available and after confirming that the patient is unresponsive and not breathing normally.

17. Turn on the AED, apply the pads to the patient's bare chest, follow the AED prompts, and deliver a shock if advised.

18. Deliver each breath over 1 second and ensure only enough air is given to make the chest visibly rise.

19. To provide a structured and effective response to cardiac arrest, improving the chances of survival and recovery.

20. Begin CPR immediately, as delays can decrease the chances of survival. It is better to err on the side of action.

EXERCISE II – ANSWERS

1. d) Assess the scene for safety

2. b) 30:2

3. c) At least 2 inches

4. b) 100-120 compressions per minute

5. c) The heel of the hand

6. b) Every 2 minutes

7. c) Begin chest compressions

8. b) Maintain blood flow to vital organs

9. b) Perform CPR immediately

10. b) Prepare the AED while compressions continue

11. b) Reposition the airway and try again

12. b) One pad on the lower left chest and the other on the upper right chest

13. b) Maintain proper depth and rate with full chest recoil

14. b) To maintain an open airway

15. a) Turn it on

16. b) Take over and provide high-quality compressions

17. b) Resume chest compressions immediately

18. d) The chest recoils fully after each compression

19. b) 1 second

20. c) A palpable pulse

<u>EXERCISE III – ANSWERS</u>

1. C) Approximately one-third the depth of the chest

2. B) 30:2

3. A) 15:2

4. D) Two fingers on the lower half of the sternum

5. B) Every 2 minutes

6. C) 100-120 compressions per minute

7. A) Neutral position with head tilt and chin lift

8. B) 12-20 breaths per minute

9. A) Turn on the AED

10. B) One pad on the chest and one on the back

11. B) Two-thumb encircling hands technique

12. B) No more than 10 seconds

13. D) Brachial artery

14. B) If the child is unresponsive and not breathing or only gasping

15. B) 10 seconds

16. B) Perform chest compressions immediately and check the mouth for the object

17. A) Lower half of the sternum

18. B) Start chest compressions

19. B) 5 back slaps

20. B) Respiratory failure or shock

EXERCISE IV – ANSWERS

1. B	8. A	15. D
2. B	9. B	16. D
3. B	10. B	17. C
4. B	11. B	18. B
5. C	12. B	19. B
6. A	13. B	20. D
7. B	14. B	

EXERRCISE V – ANSWERS

1. c	8. b	15. a
2. b	9. b	16. b
3. a	10. c	17. c
4. b	11. c	18. b
5. c	12. b	19. c
6. b	13. d	20. c
7. b	14. b	

EXERCISE VI – ANSWERS

1. b	8. c	15. b
2. b	9. b	16. b
3. c	10. d	17. c
4. b	11. b	18. b
5. b	12. a	19. a
6. b	13. a	20. c
7. b	14. b	

EXERCISE VII – ANSWERS

1. B	5. B	9. B
2. B	6. B	10. C
3. B	7. B	11. A
4. C	8. C	12. B

13. C

14. B

15. B

16. B

17. B

18. B

19. A

20. B

NOTES

NOTES

NOTES

www.ingramcontent.com/pod-product-compliance
Ingram Content Group UK Ltd.
Pitfield, Milton Keynes, MK11 3LW, UK
UKHW021407190726
13845UKWH00028B/941

9 789340 448697